Rethinking**Phonics**

Making the Best Teaching Decisions

Karin L. Dahl

Patricia L. Scharer

Lora L. Lawson

Patricia R. Grogan

HEINEMANN

Portsmouth, NH

Heinemann
A division of Reed Elsevier Inc.
361 Hanover Street
Portsmouth, NH 03801–3912
www.heinemann.com

Offices and agents throughout the world

The author and publisher wish to thank those who have generously given permission to reprint borrowed material:
"Five Fat Turkeys" reprinted with permission from *Mitt Magic: Finger Plays for Finger Puppets* by L. S. Roberts, copyright © 1985, Gryphon House, Inc., P. O. Box 207, Beltsville, MD 20704-0207.

Library of Congress Cataloging-in-Publication Data

Rethinking phonics : making the best teaching decisions / Karin L. Dahl . . . [et al.].
    p. cm.
    Includes bibliographical references and index.
    ISBN 0-325-00356-4 (pbk.)
    1. Reading—Phonetic method. 2. Language arts (Elementary). I. Dahl, Karin L., 1938–.

LB1573.3 .R48   2001
372.46'5—dc21   00-054069

Editor: Lois Bridges
Production service: Patricia Adams
Production coordination: Abigail M. Heim
Cover design: Kathy Squires
Cover image: *Open Book*, Pierre-Yves Goavec/© The Image Bank
Manufacturing: Louise Richardson

Printed in the United States of America on acid-free paper

05 04 03 02 01 RRD   2 3 4 5

To nine wonderful teachers

Contents

Acknowledgments

We deeply appreciate the collaboration and friendship of co-authorship, the love and understanding of families and friends, the advice and support of colleagues and editors, the patience and generosity of nine wonderful teachers, the feedback and suggestions of Clark County, Ohio teachers, the time and talents of thousands of other wonderful teachers who work daily to improve the future, one child at a time.

Introduction

We have written this book to help teachers see phonics instruction in terms of their own professional decision making. In our view, teachers' choices are not about which workbook to use or what pre-programmed phonics curriculum is best. Instead, teachers need to think about the letter-sound information that children need as they learn to read and write. We think that children provide the best information about what needs to be taught and what phonics concepts are within their reach. It is in working with children's actual reading and writing that the real phonics decisions for teachers become clear. These decisions require an understanding of instructional activities and strategies that link phonics with children's reading and writing. Our goal in this book is to show how teachers make informed decisions during phonics instruction and how they successfully teach phonics. The type of phonics instruction we describe is *phonics in context*. It takes into account:

- the context of children's needs and emerging phonics concepts
- the context of children's developing language knowledge
- the context of classroom reading and writing activities

We propose that phonics in context is both systematic and explicit. The more traditional version of systematic phonics involves a fixed sequence of phonics skills taught with opportunities for independent practice. Often, these traditional lessons are scripted for the teacher and involve practice sheets that deal with pictured words and matching letter-sound choices. The underlying structure of these lessons emphasizes a preset sequence of phonics concepts and intensive instruction provided by the teacher.

Critics of traditional phonics programs charge that the fixed sequence of skills may not be appropriate for some learners. One-size-fits-all phonics lessons may be too big for some, too short in the sleeves for others. Our class-room observations teach us that children first must learn that print conveys meaning before they can make sense of phonics study. Children who lack this foundation may do phonics workbook pages as teacher-assigned paper-work, marking the answers without understanding or processing the con-cepts. At the same time, other learners may already be familiar with the phonics concepts being taught. They may see the same skill exercises as busy work that keeps them from actual reading and writing.

Our research observations in classrooms have affirmed the old adage that "teaching is not a guarantee of learning." Given the range of learners in our classrooms and the complexity of their daily lives, it is highly prob-able that traditional systematic phonics may be a hit for some and a miss for others, no matter how skillfully and intensively the program is taught.

A revised view of systematic phonics is presented by Dorothy Strickland in her book *Teaching Phonics Today: A Primer for Educators* (1998). She argues that "instruction is systematic when it is planned, de-liberate in application, and proceeds in an orderly manner." She contends that this does not mean "a rigid progression of 'one-size-fits-all' instruc-tion. Rather, it means a thoughtfully planned program that takes into account learner variability" (p. 51).

The critical difference is that the learner, rather than the fixed se-quence of phonics skills, is the central consideration in instruction. Strickland argues that the "intensity of instruction on any particular skill or strategy should be based on need. Thus, intensity will vary both with individuals and groups" (p. 51).

Critics of this new notion about systematic phonics charge that skill information may be disorganized and key concepts missed. Their con-cern is about completeness of instruction when learner needs and devel-opment are the central considerations. Our research findings, however, show us that the idea of completeness needs to include not only what has been taught, but also what is learned. Children learn many concepts as they read and write each day, some outside of class, some indepen-dently, and some are developed as children read and write together.

As discussed so far, the contrast between phonics-in-context and tra-ditional phonics includes the following ideas:

PHONICS-IN-CONTEXT

1. Phonics is taught as part of reading and writing events.

2. Systematic instruction is based on learner needs and develop-ment.

3. Phonics learning comes from instruction and independent exploration.

TRADITIONAL PHONICS

1. Phonics is taught as practice in isolation. It is a stand-alone part of the curriculum.

2. Systematic instruction presents all letter-sound relations in a preset sequence.

3. Phonics learning relates to the sequence of skills taught by the teacher.

| 4. Intensive, planned instruction is designed to meet learner needs. | 4. Intensive, planned instruction provides curricular coverage of phonics skills and concepts. |

Another important finding from our research about phonics is that the best instructional activities involved are recurring ones. These ongoing classroom reading-writing activities constitute strands of daily instruction with phonics embedded. In one classroom, for example, the daily routine might be a shared reading session, then time periods for independent reading and writing workshop. The phonics-in-context lessons occur in each of these daily activities, during the teaching and discussion about a storybook, in individual conferences during independent reading, and in minilessons and work with others during writing time. These lessons, taken together and continued daily, constitute a recurring phonics curriculum for children.

Key Policies by Professional Organizations in Literacy

The debate about phonics instruction is decades old. It includes a great deal of rhetoric about how phonics should be taught and extensive political activity in the United States, resulting in many state legislatures mandating phonics instruction in schools. One of the positive outcomes of the decades-old phonics debate is that professional organizations took a role as policy leaders. The major professional organizations in reading and writing, the National Council of Teachers of English (NCTE) and the International Reading Association (IRA), have defined clear positions in the phonics debate. Their policy statements address the relative role of phonics instruction within a comprehensive reading-writing program.

The resolution adopted by the National Council of Teachers of English stated:

> that phonics for beginning as well as experienced readers is only one part of the complex, socially constructed, and cognitively demanding process called reading; that all readers need to learn a range of reading strategies, including phonics (Flanagan, 1997, p. 5).

Similarly, the policy statement from the International Reading Association emphasizes that teaching phonics is an important aspect of beginning reading instruction. It also states, "Phonics instruction, to be effective in promoting independence in reading, must be embedded in the context of a total reading/language arts program" (1997, p.1).

These policies suggest that teachers need a repertoire of phonics instructional activities that can be carried out in the context of classroom reading and writing. This repertoire of phonics instruction can serve as productive and positive alternatives to isolated phonics workbook lessons.

The main focus of this book is to describe activities that teachers can use and to provide insights into the thinking and decision making involved. Our ideas and examples come from in-depth study of phonics instruction in first-grade classrooms. We are showcasing the teaching practices that were successful in producing phonics achievement.

Meeting the Teachers

Our teacher partners in this book have a number of characteristics in common in terms of their classroom programs. Each literacy program includes:

- a child-centered approach to reading and writing,
- a wide selection of children's literature,
- sustained periods of student engagement with literacy, and
- peer collaboration during authentic reading and writing.

While all eight classroom programs share these elements, they differ in particular program emphases and thus represent a range of classroom practice. For example, our first-grade classrooms in Highland Park and Central College Elementary are primarily project-centered classrooms where children work in extended time blocks on inquiry questions that cross subject-area boundaries.

- Jenny Hootman and Beth Swanson teach collaboratively in a double first-grade class. They work through individual writing conferences, guided reading groups, and shared writing to help each child move forward in literacy learning. In their classroom, project work provides the context for student discussions, problem solving, and extended reading and writing.

- Linda Orlich teaches through projects that use literacy as a learning tool. She holds students responsible for using what they know and making reading and writing their own. During project work she focuses on individual learners and teaches through intensive daily conferences.

The classrooms at Olentangy and Emerson Elementary, in contrast, have extensive literature programs in which children engage in theme-related reading and writing.

- Lisa Dapoz uses literature study featuring a large classroom collection of books organized by genre as the heart of her instruction. Her daily time to read aloud is often followed by shared writing experiences as Lisa and her students work together to create new stories and charts to read independently.

- JoAnne Lane and her students are self-described *word detectives* as they enjoy daily readings of enlarged poems, big books, and charts of word families they have created. New insights into how words work are celebrated and decorate their room on large sheets of paper. These charts provide support for the young writers during writing workshop.

The rest of the classrooms feature particular activities that structure the daily schedule. Olde Orchard and Cline Elementary have elaborate reading and writing workshop periods and include a strong literature component.

- Janice Eddey uses consistent workshop routines to engage children in literature themes and sustained daily writing. Her lengthy individual conferences with children address needed reading and writing skills and celebrate individual progress.

- Jo Ann Abreu uses elaborate composing demonstrations during her writing workshop. These are collaborative writing events allowing the teacher and children to share the pen. Jo Ann comments that she demonstrates how to write by writing in front of her students. Her demonstrations often include talking aloud while she is writing to share her thinking.

The program emphasis at St. Luke and Grayhill Elementary varies across the year according to particular classroom activities and teachers' decisions about ways to meet the students' needs.

- Alice Pleva believes children come to value reading through modeling, so reading aloud occurs often throughout the day. She refers to this time as her *"snuggle time"* with children. She uses large group settings for reading aloud, shared reading, and shared writing, then focuses on small groups in guided reading and guided writing. Children work as partners in buddy reading and collaborative writing.

- Candace Moore demonstrates literacy thinking processes through shared writing and reading with the whole class. She focuses on specific learner's needs in individual reading and writing conferences and includes rich exposure to children's literature in her literacy instruction.

Our teacher partners will speak for themselves. Eight of the chapters include sections called *Teacher to Teacher*, featuring one particular teacher and her work. These sections include teacher advice and a description of her classroom literacy program. They provide insights into each teacher's thinking.

Looking Ahead

We've divided this book into two sections. Part One addresses foundation ideas for rethinking phonics and presenting phonics in context.

Because the central driving force for these ideas is assessment, we begin with this concept in Chapter Two. We discuss assessment strategies—from daily informal kidwatching to formal assessments. Second only to assessment as a critical concern is reaching children who struggle with reading and writing. Chapter Three features teachers' strategies for working with these children. Chapter Four covers strategies for using phonics concepts and skills when encoding or decoding text. Chapter Five describes letters, sounds, and word study. It's the chapter that looks at spelling issues and ways to teach word patterns. These chapters form the foundational aspects of connected phonics instruction.

The second section of the book addresses various instructional contexts for phonics instruction. These chapters look at ways to include phonics teaching and learning within shared reading, children's literature activities, writers' workshop, writing demonstrations, and project work. Our examples draw on the work carried out in our research classrooms. We include transcripts of conversations between teachers and students in whole group instruction, small group sessions, and individual conferences that demonstrate exactly how teachers work with children.

This book presents many ways to teach phonics that take into account the development and interests of each child—that is, instruction that builds on the principles that we outline in the first chapter. At many points throughout the book we highlight where and how teachers are making decisions. These decisions are highlighted so we can trace what teachers are choosing to do and see how their decisions work out in the interactions with children. We consider tracing teacher decision making as a key feature in our descriptions of phonics instruction.

The book as a whole presents research-based practices that have been used successfully to teach phonics in first-grade reading-writing classrooms. Within our investigation we found that the patterns of student achievement using these activities were significant, extending to learners who struggled as well as those at the top of the class.

Throughout this book we provide examples and classroom excerpts so our readers can consider their own practice and adapt ideas to their particular classrooms and students. This is a work that invites teachers to think in new ways about their phonics instruction. In these pages we show how to break the old mold of skill and drill, how to move away from workbooks and preset curricula, and how to teach phonics that connects with children's reading and writing.

Six Guiding Principles for Effective Phonics Instruction

Guiding Principles for Phonics Instruction

Six basic principles serve as key ideas to guide teacher thinking in this book. Each of these principles is accompanied by some kind of teacher challenge or dilemma. It is in answering these challenges creatively, efficiently, and effectively that the art of teaching literacy lies. We present these principles together and then describe each separately.

- Phonics knowledge is developmental.
- Phonics instruction is integrated into beginning reading and writing instruction.
- Phonics knowledge is important not for itself but in its application.
- Strategic knowledge is required to use phonics concepts and skills.
- Phonics instruction involves teacher decision making.
- Peers teach each other phonics as they read and write side-by-side.

Principle 1: Phonics Knowledge Is Developmental

Phonics knowledge is related to children's evolving written language knowledge and their individual efforts to learn. Although there are some identifiable general trajectories along which children tend to develop, each child's development is different. The dilemma for the teacher is how to scaffold the child appropriately, and most importantly, how to connect with each learner. How much of a challenge can a given student accept? Where is the frustration level of each learner? What is the next step for a particular child? We do not believe that one-size-fits-all in phonics instruction.

This instructional connection takes into account the idea that teacher assistance at critical moments can help children bridge the gap between the known and unknown. It suggests that teachers match phonics instruction to the developmental needs of the individual child. They use classroom management techniques to assess and teach to the needs of each child and also cope with a wide range of learners.

Principle 2: Phonics Instruction Is Integrated into Beginning Reading and Writing Instruction

Phonics instruction is a key part of the beginning curriculum in reading and writing but we do not see it as a prerequisite. There are important understandings about letters and sounds that go hand-in-hand with progress in reading and writing and that develop in tandem with children's grasp of reading and writing as meaning-centered processes. We want children to make the key phonics concepts their own and not have critical gaps in this basic area of knowledge. The challenge is to ensure children have access to the full range of phonics knowledge and to ensure that phonics teaching relates developmentally to the reading and writing they are doing. Our research experience showed that over the course of the school year, this full range of information was apparent in all the classrooms we studied; the order in which individual children worked with given concepts differed according to the child's needs.

Principle 3: Phonics Knowledge Is Important Not for Itself But in Its Application

It is phonics in use that children need to understand. Children use letter-sound knowledge along with their knowledge of syntax and semantics in order to read and write. Phonics instruction needs to help children see this connection—it needs to be clear in children's minds that we use letter-sound concepts as we read and write. This means that any separate phonics instruction must include some connection to meaningful text and to the acts of reading and writing. Teachers working with this idea keep finding new ways of bringing phonics into a range of classroom activities.

This connection also supports what is known about processes of meaning making and their centrality to literacy learning. Literacy is primarily a means of communication. Just as spoken language is acquired in meaningful contexts, so literacy is acquired in the same way. The teachers presented in this book help children use phonics information while making sense of print and creating their own written messages.

Principle 4: Strategic Knowledge Is Required to Use Phonics Concepts and Skills

From the beginning children need to learn some clear routines for looking at written text and mobilizing their phonics knowledge to check a word, rethink a spelling, or reread a sentence. Strategic knowledge needs to be interwoven with phonics concepts and skills to ensure application. Classroom literacy work involves not just instructing about phonics concepts but also how to use those concepts in the process of reading and writing. This instruction helps children understand both the *what* and the *how* of reading and writing. These strategies are explained directly and clearly, they are demonstrated again and again, and children receive individual instruction in how to use them as particular problems arise. The challenge of strategy instruction for teachers is to examine many kinds of reading and writing to make these strategies and their use clear, to provide whole group and small group practice at using these strategies, and to support individual students in taking up and using the strategies effectively.

Principle 5: Phonics Instruction Involves Teacher Decision Making

This connection suggests that phonics instruction is assessment driven. The information gained about a particular student's learning is an essential key to the subsequent instruction. Teachers make decisions about which phonics information and strategies to teach to particular learners and when to teach it. Instruction is often tailor-made to specific children and appropriate to their developmental needs. Our research shows that teachers connect their phonics instruction to three kinds of knowledge as they make these decisions:

1. They consider the concepts that must be learned. This body of phonics knowledge essentially serves as their guiding internal curriculum to shape their questions and observations of learners.

2. Teachers also connect their sense of what each child has been working on lately with the concepts and skills that are within reach. They know which phonics concepts and skills have been talked about in lessons and what is emerging in daily reading and writing.

3. They see inherent phonics instructional opportunities in the work of the moment—the skills, concepts, and strategies that are teaching opportunities in the book or student's draft at hand.

The challenge for teachers is to discern for each child the next instructional steps to be made, and then to find a way of taking those steps in the context of individual work, small group work, large group work, or peer instruction.

Principle 6: Peers Teach Each Other Phonics as They Read and Write Side-by-Side

Phonics instruction is present in the peer interactions of children at work reading and writing as well as in teacher-student work. Children learn from each other as they read and write side-by-side. The social context of the reading-writing classroom is a factor instructionally in the phonics program. The dilemma for teachers is figuring out how to make the most of the social contexts of literacy in the process of teaching literacy concepts and strategies.

Glimpses of Instruction

To see how these principles work in real classrooms, we turn to a sampling of quick lessons with four teachers. The point is to demonstrate phonics instruction in the context of reading and writing activities. We illustrate the kinds of teacher actions that are involved. Three different kinds of phonics instruction are included in this sampling: group reading-writing activities, individual phonics instruction, and inductive lessons. The classroom examples are taken from classroom transcripts (with fictitious names for children). We present them as if we are visiting in each classroom, watching the teacher and students at work.

1. Group Reading-Writing Activities with Phonics Embedded

We begin by visiting a parochial school, St. Luke Elementary, where the first-grade class is looking at a poem written in large letters on chart paper. Their teacher, Alice Pleva, has children working on phonological awareness to develop the ability to hear and manipulate the sound units of language. The usual routine for such lessons begins with children reading and talking about a book or poem. Then the teacher invites children to look at the written text and listen closely as she reads in order to find rhyming pairs or words with particular patterns. The sounds of the rhyme or the word patterns they identify form the heart of the group discussion.

The children are working with a poem "Five Fat Turkeys" (Roberts, 1985) and looking closely at the written text.

> Five fat turkeys
> Sitting on a gate.
> The first one said,
> "Oh, my, it's getting late!"
> The second one said,
> "Thanksgiving is near."
> The third one said, "that makes me shake with fear."

They read the poem together, then Mrs. Pleva asks children to listen as she reads the poem by herself from the chart. The children notice various rhymes and the teacher responds.

MRS. PLEVA: Yes, there's a rhyming pattern in this poem. Who will come up and frame two words that rhyme?

CHARLES: (Walks up to the chart and frames *gate* and *late*.)

MRS. PLEVA: Charles, say the two words you framed.

CHARLES: *Gate, late*.

MRS. PLEVA: What do these two words do?

CHARLES: Sound the same.

MRS. PLEVA: Where do they sound the same? At the beginning or the ending?

CHARLES: The ending.

The lesson continues as other rhyming pairs are framed by children putting their hands on each side of the word and reading aloud. Mrs. Pleva goes on to reinforce the concept of seeing and hearing rhyming patterns at the ends of words.

This lesson shows a foundational phonics concept experienced and then woven into the study of a poem. The children participate and identify patterns as part of their shared reading activity. They also enjoy the poem as a whole on its own.

In a similar fashion, shared writing activities are often the context for phonics instruction as children talk about the spellings of words to be written. These group lessons can focus on hearing and representing sounds in sequence as a piece of writing is generated. A visit to Grayhill Elementary, an inner-city school, shows what this instruction looks like.

Candace Moore leads the class each day in writing Our Daily News, a report of classroom news and events. The teacher writes the child-dictated sentences on chart paper tacked to the front chalkboard. This instructional activity, with the teacher as scribe, emphasizes phonemic segmentation (recognizing the sounds of each phoneme in sequence and representing them with appropriate letters) and includes a running teacher commentary about specific letter-sound relationships within children's dictated words. Mrs. Moore shows how to represent intended meaning as she writes each word.

Children have suggested the third sentence of the daily news: *Today Lauren and Mackenzie read a book*. They have worked on all the words and now are ready to work on the word *book*.

MRS. MOORE: *Book*. Get us started, *b-oo-k*.

LAUREN: *B*

MRS. MOORE: (Writes *B*.) Who can tell me some other letters? Don't give me the ending. We need something in between, *b-OO-k*.

ANN: *O*

MACKENZIE: *C*

MRS. MOORE: No *C* in it.

RASHANA: *K*

MRS. MOORE: It has two *O*s in it, then the *K*. (Writes *O O K*). These two *O*s say *oo*. (She makes the appropriate *O* sound and points to the two *O*s.) Can you say it?

CHILDREN: *oo*

MRS. MOORE: Good.

The lesson continues as other words are written sound-by-sound and then the class reads the text as a whole. Often these lessons are followed by the game *I Spy*. Mrs. Moore asks children to find words with consonant blends or a particular vowel pattern. This game reinforces the letter-sound relationships that were just used in shared writing.

2. Individual Phonics Instruction

In contrast to these whole group lessons, the teacher also works with children one-at-a-time providing instruction about the particular phonics concepts children need in writing or reading.

A visit to an individual reading conference at Central College Elementary, a language arts magnet school, shows this reinforcement. Here, Linda Orlich, a teacher who works extensively with individual learners each day, is looking closely at one student's strategies.

Daniel is midway through *At the Zoo* (1979) and is reading the sentence, *Five tigers clawing*, to his teacher.

DANIEL: Four tigers scratch.

MRS. ORLICH: That's what the picture shows. (She then points to the word *clawing* and keeps her finger there.)

DANIEL: *C, L, c-l* (pauses).

MRS. ORLICH: What does *A W* say? *aw*

DANIEL: *Cl-aw*, four tigers clawing.

MRS. ORLICH: Look at the picture.

DANIEL: (Looks at the illustration of five tigers and then back at the word *five*.)

Daniel does not correct his miscue at this point.

In this conference, Mrs. Orlich emphasizes various kinds of information in addition to letter-sound relations. The phonics concept is emphasized along with the meaning represented in both illustration and text. Working in this way through several pages, she helps Daniel begin to self-correct.

3. Inductive Group Activities

Inductive activities emphasizing word analysis place children in the role of discovering and discussing words that fit specific letter-sound patterns. Teachers ask questions and help children talk about the evidence they gather. At suburban Olentangy Elementary, JoAnne Lane's class is reading some favorite chart poems just before Thanksgiving. The children notice that the lines of one poem end with rhyming words like *see, tree, be, me,* and *turkey*. This discovery is the beginning of the class' work to generate more words with the same rhyming sound. As they write the words and discover more than one spelling pattern, they group words together and Mrs. Lane writes each word family on a large paper tee shirt. The shirts are then added to the growing collection of paper laundry hanging from the clothesline along the wall filled with similar shirts—each depicting a word family. As the year progresses, the class adds new words to each shirt and more tee shirts with new word families to their clothesline. These lessons connect word patterns to other poems the children read and to stories the children write independently.

In other instruction, knowledge of consonants and vowels is developed as children brainstorm words having a specific beginning sound or a certain vowel pattern. Chart paper lists created during these lessons are displayed on classroom walls, documenting ongoing consonant and vowel instruction. The lists also serve as resources for children during independent writing.

Basic Definitions

These brief examples present phonics instruction in which children are working with meaningful text or are preparing to read or write independently. The phonics concepts are identified and explained but are not isolated from the reading and writing processes. Clearly, our definition of phonics for these lessons and throughout the book is an inclusive one. It encompasses foundational skills such as phonological awareness, phonemic awareness, and phonemic segmentation as well as the concepts and strategies needed to use letter-sound relationships and patterns in reading and writing. These are essential terms for our discussion of phonics. We draw on the careful work of Michael Opitz in *Rhymes and Reasons: Literature and Language Play for Phonological Awareness* (2000) for these key definitions.

DEFINITION OF KEY TERMS
- *Phonological awareness* refers to awareness of many aspects of spoken language. These include the awareness of the following basic sound units:

    Words within sentences

    Syllables within words

    Phonemes within syllables and words
- *Phonemic awareness* refers to the awareness that words are made up of individual sounds. It is one aspect of the larger category of phonological awareness.
- *Phoneme segmentation* refers to isolating sounds at the beginning of a word or in an entire word. Sometimes the task requires hearing and counting; other times it requires producing actual sounds.

(pp. 5–7)

Key Questions and Answers

Phonics instruction involves day-by-day decision making. Our inquiry into this decision making process has been guided by several broad questions:

- What does phonics instruction look like in classrooms where teachers have rich literature programs for reading instruction and daily writing experiences for young children?

- What do the teachers in such programs say and do as they teach phonics?

- How do teachers keep phonics instruction connected to reading and writing?

- What options can teachers use to reach the children who have particular difficulty with phonics concepts?

- How do teachers connect phonics instruction with shared reading, project work, writing workshop, writing demonstrations, and daily literature study?

- What assessment strategies do teachers use to look at phonics learning and growth?

- What is the interplay between explicit phonics teaching and more implicit embedded phonics instruction?

- What information guides teacher decision making as teachers rethink their phonics programs from day to day?

The answers to these questions came from our partnership with first-grade teachers in process-centered classrooms. Their instructional answers are effective and have a track record linked to achievement.

Throughout this book we present the teaching practices of nine teachers who have been particularly successful across a wide range of learners. Their success is demonstrated by children's achievement in phonics concepts as well as children's engagement with literacy. In each of their classrooms we studied how phonics instruction took place, what was taught, and what children learned about phonics during first grade. We observed in their classrooms weekly throughout the year, recorded phonics instruction, and documented student achievement (Dahl *et al.*, 1999, Dahl and Scharer, 2000).

The Importance of a Literate Environment

Each of the classrooms described in this book is a literate environment. The classrooms feature accessible print that supports children's daily reading and writing. Each classroom has a sizeable library of children's books, with featured authors and books available in groupings. Each uses chart poems, lists, and big books for instruction. The walls include displays of children's work showcasing their writing and lists from word study. Various posters and charts support particular strategies and list procedures to remember in reading-writing activities. There are words from recent group study posted on the walls and abundant print from which children can learn. The literate environment functions as a support system for children. It provides resources and prompts that celebrate and encourage literate behavior.

Summary

The principles for phonics instruction guiding this book suggest that teachers make key decisions as they teach. They look closely at learners and at learning opportunities. Their instruction involves careful consideration of the basic phonics concepts, skills, and strategies that children need. And they think about how to connect instruction with children's developing literacy. This book deals with making informed decisions about phonics teaching in the primary grades. Our central purpose is to help teachers see instructional options as they work with letter-sound relationships. Throughout this book we show decision points as teachers interact with children. The phonics teaching described is connected to the main reading and writing activities that take place in primary grade reading and writing programs. These include shared reading, guided reading, literature study, word study, writing workshop, writing demonstrations, and project work. There is a chapter for each of these activities. We begin with foundation concerns including assessment, working with strugglers, strategy instruction, and word study. Then we show phonics instruction in the context of specific reading and writing activities.

2

How Assessment
Informs Instruction

Each afternoon in JoAnne Lane's classroom begins with a quiet independent reading time when children enjoy reading and rereading their favorite books. Mrs. Lane is listening to Sara read her story and is taking a running record as Sara reads. A running record is a quick written record of a child's actual reading. Check marks represent words read correctly. Words read differently than the text are noted along with the child's self-corrections and other reading behaviors. During her reading, Sara hesitates at the word *clue*.

MRS. LANE: Remember the consonant blend *C L*?

SARA: *cl*?

MRS. LANE: Yes, and the rest of the word is a long *U* sound since there's an *E* at the end.

SARA: *u*

MRS. LANE: Good. Now put it together.

SARA: *clue*.

MRS. LANE: Now read the whole sentence.

As she listens to Sara finish the book, Mrs. Lane notes that Sara uses the pattern of the first few pages to help read more fluently later in the story and independently uses another consonant blend to read an unfamiliar word, *crunch*. After the story Mrs. Lane encourages Sara to continue using helpful reading strategies saying, "I like the way that you were rereading and getting your mouth ready to use the sounds at the beginning of the words. You are doing all the right things. Good job."

Reading conferences such as this provide important information for teachers like Mrs. Lane as they observe children and the ways they use phonics to read unfamiliar words. As Sara read, Mrs. Lane documented both the assistance she provided when Sara struggled with a word, and Sara's independent use of letter-sound relationships later in the story to read a new word.

In this chapter, we describe the patterns of assessment used as teachers purposefully and intentionally learned and recorded information about the phonics knowledge and literacy development of their students. Our analysis revealed three consistent patterns of teachers' efforts to identify the strengths of their students, to match instruction appropriately with student need, and move children along as readers and writers:

- Teachers are engaged in daily and periodic assessment techniques to learn about their students' knowledge of phonics concepts and literacy understandings.
- Teachers used this knowledge to plan instruction to meet the needs of their students.
- The cycle of student assessment, instructional decision making, and purposeful instruction continued throughout the year.

These three findings are key concepts to the discussion of student assessment in this chapter, which explores the relationships between assessment, instruction, children, and teachers during the teaching and learning of phonics. We know that by focusing on the strengths of students, teachers have a foundation from which to work. Existing knowledge serves as connections for new knowledge.

Teaching to Meet Individual Needs

During each day of data collection, we observed teachers learning about their students and planning instruction to meet the needs of individuals in their classrooms. The teachers' ability to hold a clear understanding of each child as a reader and writer is an essential component of their teaching. In addition, teachers must use their knowledge of literacy development to know which concept best supports the young reader and writer. Assessments help teachers know which children are just beginning to connect letters and sounds, which children control beginning and ending consonants, which children are working on short vowels, and which children are moving into more complex phonics understandings. This information influences the instructional decisions teachers make as they plan large group lessons, as they meet with individual students during reading or writing conferences, and as they select small groups of children for a particular lesson.

The intent behind daily and periodic assessments is to adjust instruction according to student need. The emphasis is on the child, as the teacher determines the timing and sequence of lessons. The teachers make instructional decisions by looking for similarities and contrasts across students. They look at how children progress as readers and writers developmentally and use various kinds of activities as instructional tools. These activities include:

- shared reading—a large group reading of a story, chart, or poem with the teacher guiding story understanding and concept development
- guided reading— small group of children with similar abilities reading a book where the teacher-led discussion focuses on children's strategies and comprehension

- writers workshop—sustained writing time with support for children's developing writing processes, workshops often begin with mini-lessons and end with group sharing
- word study—vocabulary, phonics, and spelling concepts studied by looking for patterns and relationships
- shared writing—teachers and students produce a jointly constructed text and the teacher serves as scribe to record ideas and discuss word features

Based on those factors, they select the appropriate instructional context and focus of each lesson to help children learn how words work. Teachers' goals are to know each child as a reader and writer so they can plan effective instruction. They use a variety of assessments throughout the school year

- to understand the phonics knowledge of each student,
- to document shifts in phonics knowledge,
- to help describe spelling and phonics progress on grade cards,
- and to design future lessons.

How teachers approach these goals is both intensive and systematic. It is intensive in that assessment occurs every day adding to teachers' understanding of their students. It is systematic as daily assessments are documented and then linked with periodic assessments to create a larger picture of student understanding and shifts in learning over time.

This chapter is organized in terms of both approaches. First, the daily assessments teachers use will be described as an essential thread in the fabric of each day, weaving in and out of teachers' instructional decisions. Next, the periodic assessments teachers use regularly throughout the year will be described as ways to extend and strengthen teachers' daily documentation of student learning.

How Teachers Document Phonics Learning Each Day

Four tools can be used to assess students' phonics knowledge each day: kidwatching, running records, reading conferences, and writing conferences. Across the language arts instructional time, these four tools combine to provide extensive opportunities for teachers to document students' progress.

Kidwatching

Yetta Goodman first coined the term *kidwatching* to describe what teachers do as they carefully observe students throughout the day (Goodman, 1985). Kidwatching is much more than looking at children as they work in the classroom. It involves ongoing observation and, most importantly, consistent interpretation as teachers ask, "What can I learn about this child?" and "What should I do next to help this student learn?" These questions help teachers translate observations into knowledge about children's current understandings about phonics and students' approaches to learning about letters and sounds, so they can make instructional decisions about how to use that knowledge to accelerate student achievement.

Kidwatching begins on the first day of school and continues every day throughout the year. Candace Moore describes her efforts to learn about her students' knowledge of letters and sounds by explaining that, "I observe the children at the beginning of the year when I first start out with the class and I try to find out what they remember from kindergarten." Mrs. Moore's observations help her decide where instruction should begin with her new group of students. Team teachers, Beth Swanson and Jenny Hootman, agree. "We look at the children's needs and their past experiences and what they're coming to know. And then we take them on from there."

Mrs. Swanson and Mrs. Hootman further describe the importance of watching children as they write independently because "actually seeing the children and listening and observing children is a really powerful lesson because you see the confusion that they have, and also their knowledge as they write." Critical information about each child's understanding of letters and sounds is revealed as Mrs. Swanson and Mrs. Hootman watch children write their messages. They listen and take notes as children discuss their daily journal entries or writing workshop stories during conferences.

Kidwatching takes place throughout the day in both large and small group contexts. Each of the following instructional events provides unique opportunities to learn about students' phonics knowledge.

- Reading aloud—How do children get involved with the story? Do they chime in on rhyming refrains? Do they understand if the author is playing with sounds and words? Do they become involved in predicting the next part of an ABC book using letters and sounds?

- Shared reading—How do they use the print to participate in the shared reading? Are they using first letters, word patterns, or word parts to read unknown words? Are they noticing word patterns in the story and using that information to read more fluently?

- Guided reading—How do children respond to unknown words? Do they use the letter-sound concepts they know to actively figure out new words? Do they make connections between known and unknown words?

- Shared writing—How do children help the teacher write the message? Do they provide appropriate suggestions about letters to

represent sounds or word patterns? Do they make connections
between print around the room such as name charts, word families,
or other writing projects and their own writing?

- Independent writing—How do children attempt to write unfamiliar
  words? Are they using initial or final consonants, names of letters,
  or more complex phonics concepts? What do they do to help
  themselves—refer to print around the room, say the word slowly,
  ask a friend, consult a personal dictionary, or find the word in a
  book?

Each of these kidwatching opportunities contributes to the constantly
changing picture that teachers hold of students' phonics understanding
and how it applies to their reading and writing. Mrs. Lane's kidwatching
checklist is a way to quickly record observations and note changes over
time. Some teachers write down their observations on sticky notes, record
sheets, or student files as they watch children work; other observations
are held in the teacher's memory, linked with new observations, and used
to decide on the next teaching point.

KIDWATCHING CHECKLIST
Talks to a friend about writing

Rereads writing

Looks in books

Looks in the dictionary

Looks at walls or charts

Sounds out words aloud

Helps someone else spell a word

Asks a friend for help in spelling

Waits for the teacher to help

Reverts to pictures

Puts work away in frustration

Uses placeholders

Running Records

Teachers use running records to further document children's phonics
knowledge by listening to individual children read and creating a written record of the reading, like a tape-recording on paper. Using a combination of check marks for accurate reading and other symbols to mark
errors, repetitions, and attempts at unknown words, teachers record everything a child says while reading. Running records help teachers understand students' phonics knowledge within the context of reading

stories. For example, if a reader stops at the word *batting* while reading a story about baseball, the running record documents if the child used the first letter of the word, identified known chunks of letters (*at, bat,* or *ing*), or moved from left to right using letters and sounds to figure out the word. Every attempt is recorded on the running record. Errors also provide useful information. If, for example, the child reads *throwing* instead of *batting* and consistently ignores the letters of other unknown words, the teacher focuses instruction on helping the child learn that using what they know about letters and sounds will help them read with greater accuracy. (For additional information about running records, see Clay's *An Observation Survey of Early Literacy Achievement,* 1993.)

Following the running record, teachers can respond immediately to support and clarify students' phonics understandings. If, for example, the child has consistently ignored the initial sound of words substituting *lions* for *tigers,* the teacher can direct the child back to the words documented in the running record and provide teaching points such as: "You read '*I see the lions.*' What would you expect to see at the beginning of *lions*? Could this word be *lions*? Use the first letter. Get your mouth ready. What else could it be?" Such on-the-spot instruction teaches children to attend more closely to initial sounds and supports their application of phonics concepts as they read.

Teachers take running records while children are reading a variety of texts during many different contexts such as the following:

- during sustained reading time while the child is reading a familiar story
- during a small group guided reading lesson while the child reads a new book or one previously introduced
- during reading conferences while the child reads a book of his/her choice
- during reading conferences while the child reads a book the teacher has selected

Each of these contexts provides a slightly different piece of information about a child's phonics knowledge. The running record should note whether the teacher or child selected the book and if it is a new text or familiar one (because familiar stories may be read with fewer errors and greater fluency). Greater insight into phonics knowledge may be gained when children read new stories and encounter more unfamiliar words. By analyzing running records while listening to a child read and periodically examining that child's records over time, teachers can:

- See if texts are too easy or too difficult.
- Help select new books for independent reading and instruction.
- Check on strategies readers use to read unfamiliar words.

- Look for patterns in children's attempts and respond instructionally.
- Document changes in levels of books students can read independently.

Reading Conferences

Reading conferences are individual meetings between the teacher and student that help teachers focus attention on one child, document the child's reading behaviors, and provide an opportunity for on-the-spot instruction. Lisa Dapoz organizes her schedule so she can listen to three or four children read each day. She meets with every child on a regular basis but often provides extra individual time for students who are experiencing some difficulty learning to read.

Teachers may take running records during reading conferences but may also record other observations to help them keep track of students' progress. Information gathered beyond a running record may include a retelling of the story or description of the reader's fluency.

The following example is taken from a typical reading conference in Mrs. Lane's classroom. It illustrates the important information the teacher gains while documenting one child's reading and the rich opportunities for on-the-spot instruction that help to move the child ahead as a reader.

Mrs. Lane invites Emily to the reading table and introduces a small book about a bear. During the conference, Mrs. Lane notices that Emily consistently shakes her head when she comes to an unknown word and does not make an audible attempt.

> **DECISION**: Encourage Emily to think about what would make sense in the story, to go back to the beginning of the sentence, and to get her mouth ready to say the word.

The teacher's prompts help Emily read words successfully and provide important strategies, which she uses independently later in the book to read new words. Toward the end of the story, Emily struggles with the word *raggedy* until she slides her finger under each letter softly saying each sound.

EMILY: Every letter seems to make sense. I guess that's a raggedy doll.

> **DECISION**: Reinforce the strategies Emily has demonstrated to read unfamiliar words and confirm her efforts to use picture cues and letter-sound relationships.

MRS. LANE: And that's exactly right. You used picture cues that could help you and you used the letter sounds. I saw you getting your mouth ready here and you went through each sound. You remembered short *A* and the *G* sound. And, you remembered the *Y* at the end says *E*. And then you looked at the picture again and you are right; it is *raggedy*. So, that was wonderful.

EMILY: I thought it might be Raggedy Ann or raggedy doll, or something like that.

The conference continues as Mrs. Lane asks Emily to tell her about the story. Emily replies, "The boy was looking for his bear, and he found lots of other toys. They helped him find the bear and the bear read everyone a story." In closing, Mrs. Lane re-emphasizes the way that Emily uses beginning sounds, identifies chunks of words, and works at new words until they make sense in the story. Within the context of a 10-minute conference, Mrs. Lane learns a great deal about Emily as a reader and Emily learns to apply some helpful strategies for reading unfamiliar words.

Writing Conferences

Writing conferences may range from quick exchanges as the teacher moves about the class during writer's workshop and notes progress on the child's current writing project, to more extended conferences about pieces nearly finished. Mrs. Lane initiates brief writing conferences by moving to where the child is writing and asking the child to tell her about the story. She finds that this retelling of the story helps hold the child's ideas in place as they write longer and longer messages. The exchange also provides her with a chance to note the difficulties the child may be experiencing while writing and to offer immediate instruction to help move the child into what their class calls *library spellings* or conventional spellings.

Some conferences are called to provide specific instruction based on the child's current work or needs the teacher has previously identified. Janice Eddey, for example, noticed that Kelsey was starting to say words slowly and write what she was hearing. The teacher wanted to build on Kelsey's early attempts and requested an editing conference to work on her story about giving cookies to her cousin's babies. As Kelsey rereads her story, they notice that she left the words *of them* off the end of her sentence. She has written, *We eat all.*

DECISION: Help Kelsey revisit her text and complete the sentence.

KELSEY: I know how to spell *of*. It's easy. (Writes *O*.)

MRS. EDDEY: Of them. Get your mouth ready to say *the ee-mm*.

KELSEY: (Writes *thed*.)

> **DECISION**: Emphasize saying the word slowly and checking your writing to see if you have represented all of the sounds you hear correctly.

MRS. EDDEY: Can I ask you why you put a *D* at the end? Say *them* to yourself.

KELSEY: Oh! (She is aware of the ending sound.)

MRS. EDDEY: What letter do you hear at the end?

KELSEY: *M*. (Writes *M*.)

To close the conference, Mrs. Eddey recognizes and celebrates the work Kelsey has done stretching out sounds. Mrs. Eddey asks, "Are you becoming a better writer because you're putting all those sounds down on your paper?" Kelsey's reply is a very proud nod of agreement.

Conferences are also times for teachers to continually raise expectations about the quality of student work. Lisa Dapoz believes that "at the beginning [of the year] I would pretty much accept anything that was written down, especially if they had the beginning and ending sounds. I didn't worry a whole lot about what was in the middle. Now, they're getting into looking up words in their personal dictionaries, and I'm just a lot pickier about their spelling now, toward the middle and end of the year." As the year progresses, Mrs. Dapoz shifts her expectations for individual children according to the developmental level of each child. She constantly moves them toward conventional spellings while simultaneously encouraging children to attempt new and more difficult words. The child's spelling of *cake* as *kak* may reflect the child's current strategy of using the names of the letters to spell unfamiliar words. This attempt may reflect the child's new learning of saying the word slowly and writing down what you hear. Later in the year, however, as the child learns more about long vowel patterns, Mrs. Dapoz expects to see *cake* spelled conventionally. Similarly, as high-frequency words like *the*, *is*, *and*, and *with* are studied during shared reading, shared writing, and interactive writing, Mrs. Dapoz expects to see a greater number of students spelling such words quickly and correctly. By meeting regularly with individual writers, teachers can keep track of new learning the children demonstrate in their writing and also provide important tailor-made instruction to move children ahead to more complex spellings.

How Teachers Use Periodic Assessments to Document Phonics Knowledge

In addition to daily assessments of phonics concepts, teachers can schedule specific periodic assessments aimed at taking a methodical look at the progress of each child in the class. These assessments tend to be more formal than the daily assessments and are scheduled at a variety of intervals: the beginning and end of the year, monthly, or toward the end of each grading period. Periodic assessments may involve analyzing student writing, using formal spelling assessments, documenting children's reading of benchmark books, using the Names Test (Cunningham, 1990), or completing all or part of the Observation Survey (Clay, 1993).

Systematic Analysis of Student Writing

Each month Mrs. Lane studies samples of each student's writing, looking for patterns of change. The assessment form she developed in Table 2-1 enables her to document students' control over spelling features such as consonants, vowels, and suffixes. She also examines the samples to note the percentage of conventionally spelled words found in each sample. Over time, she compares each sample with the previous month to determine progress in writing independently. The time she spends analyzing student's writing complements her daily observations of their work and her documentation during writing conferences. It provides an important time of reflection about each child and the class as a whole. What she learns about her students helps her plan minilessons for the entire class and provides further insights into individual student's progress.

Other teachers organize student writing in portfolios and compare early and late samples each grading period. This analysis helps the teacher complete grade cards, checklists, and anecdotal records for parents. Teachers also find common threads between portfolios that help them plan future minilessons or individual conferences. In Mrs. Dapoz's room, the children complete their own analysis of their writing portfolios as they prepare for student-led conferences with their parents. Mrs. Dapoz's first graders become articulate experts as they explain what they have learned about letters, sounds, and words to their parents and discuss changes in their writing over time.

Spelling Assessments

Teachers can find a variety of spelling assessments in two recent professional books: *Words Their Way: Word Study for Phonics, Vocabulary, and Spelling Instruction* (Bear *et al.*, 2000) and *Word Journeys: Assessment-Guided Phonics, Spelling, and Vocabulary Instruction* (Ganske, 2000). Several useful spelling inventories are part of the appendix in *Words Their Way*. Each inventory has a specific audience and purpose. In *Words Their Way*, The Elementary Spelling Inventory (p. 288) is a list of 25 words selected to help teachers complete a quick assessment of a child's knowledge about spelling. Teachers dictate groups of five increasingly more difficult words and stop the test when the child misses three out of five words. Feature guides are included that help teachers identify students' knowledge of

TABLE 2-1   Writing Samples: Monthly Analysis

Child's Name: _____   Dates Collected: _____

Analysis Scale
C = *the child has control; consistent use*
D = *the child is developing this concept; inconsistent use*
I = *no evidence; no use or randomly used; no pattern*

	SEP	OCT	NOV	DEC	JAN	FEB	MAR	APR	MAY
CONSONANTS									
Initial	–	–	–	–	–	–	–	–	–
Final	–	–	–	–	–	–	–	–	–
VOWELS									
Short	–	–	–	–	–	–	–	–	–
Long	–	–	–	–	–	–	–	–	–
Combinations	–	–	–	–	–	–	–	–	–
SUFFIXES									
-ed	–	–	–	–	–	–	–	–	–
-ing	–	–	–	–	–	–	–	–	–
-s (es)	–	–	–	–	–	–	–	–	–
% OF INVENTED SPELLING	–	–	–	–	–	–	–	–	–
% OF CONVENTIONAL SPELLING	–	–	–	–	–	–	–	–	–

JoAnne Lane, Olentangy Elementary School

specific spelling concepts. Also from *Words Their Way*, teachers can use the Primary Spelling Inventory (p. 295) or Upper Grade Spelling Inventory (p. 297) for similar information in greater depth.

Ganske's *Word Journeys* offers teachers four lists of spelling words specifically designed to determine a child's developmental spelling level. Lists are based upon progressively more difficult phonics concepts. The first list (Letter Name), for example, has one-syllable words with simple consonant and short vowel patterns. Words on the second list (Within Word) are also only one syllable but the list includes more complicated consonant and vowel patterns. The final two lists (Syllable Juncture and Derivational Constancy) involve multi-syllabic words with more complex spelling patterns. Teachers can use Ganske's Screening Inventory as a quick way to determine which of the four lists is most appropriate for each child. Then, by analyzing children's spellings for each list, teachers can determine which spelling features children know and which should be the focus for instruction.

Benchmark Books

The use of benchmark books is related to Clay's Text Reading Level (TRL) task in that children read unfamiliar stories and teachers record reading behaviors. During TRL, children read progressively more difficult texts until they read two books with accuracy below 90 percent. The last level read at 90 percent or above is considered their instructional level. Benchmark testing, however, involves a smaller number of texts; each assigned to a particular time of year. In January, for example, all children in the class are asked to read the same book and the teacher notes if they read with an accuracy at or above 90 percent. Those reading the book with a high level of accuracy do not progress to another level of task—the intent behind the benchmark books is to see how many children can achieve an identified standard and not to identify levels beyond that standard. Benchmark books can be used at the end of each grading period to document shifts in learning or to identify children who need additional support in meeting that particular level of achievement.

Names Test

The Names Test (Cunningham, 1990) is an easy way for teachers to learn about the decoding skills of students in grade two and beyond. As children individually read a series of first and last names, the teacher records both accurate reading and attempts. Scoring determines the number of errors made while reading initial consonants and blends, consonant digraphs, and a variety of vowel patterns. By using this test, teachers can easily identify the phonics features children already control while decoding. This avoids wasting time teaching known features so teachers can plan for instruction on more difficult phonics concepts.

Observation Survey

Clay's Observation Survey offers six tools for documenting early reading achievement. Four of the tools are particularly useful ways to assess knowledge of letters and sounds. The Letter Identification task is an efficient way to note children's level of knowledge about letter names. Children are asked to write two sentences in the Hearing and Recording Sounds in Words task; they are given credit for each of the 37 phonemes they accurately represent.

Additional information about children's spellings can be gained through the Writing Vocabulary task as children are prompted to write as many words as they can in 10 minutes. Finally, children's application of phonics knowledge while reading is documented as the teacher takes running records on a set of increasingly more difficult unfamiliar texts during the Text Reading Level task. Text Reading Levels used in Reading Recovery range from Level 0 (preprimer) to Level 30 (grade 6).

Clay (1993) provides forms for each task that document student knowledge and changes in student learning over time when the task is repeated throughout the year. In addition, results of each task can be combined and analyzed to strengthen the teacher's understanding of each student's knowledge of letter-sound relationships.

Phonics Assessment in One Classroom

Each of the assessments described in this chapter offer insight into children's phonics knowledge that enable teachers to target instruction to meet individual needs. How teachers might combine these assessments into a comprehensive plan can be understood by a visit to Highland Park. Beth Swanson and Jenny Hootman use a combination of assessments in their shared first-grade classroom of 50 students. At the beginning of the school year, Mrs. Swanson and Mrs. Hootman complete a district-mandated testing that includes the following:

- letter identification
- sentence dictation task
- writing words for ten minutes
- running records on specific books
- writing sample

Results of these assessments help them identify phonics concepts to emphasize in large instruction during shared reading and writing activities. The assessments also help them plan minilessons at the beginning of writer's workshop and teaching points during writing conferences. They repeat the same assessments at the end of the year.

Assessment scores also help the teachers make decisions about small group work. They will use guided reading groups to work on reading and focus on specific phonics features. As the small groups meet, Mrs. Hootman and Mrs. Swanson continue to take running records while individuals read; they also note the ways readers are using the phonics concepts as they attempt unknown words. Membership in the small groups changes as children progress based on what Mrs. Hootman and Mrs. Swanson learn about their students while listening to them read.

Just before grade cards each quarter, Mrs. Swanson and Mrs. Hootman use a combination of several assessments such as the following:

- spelling lists created by their teaching staff
- sight vocabulary list
- samples from each child's writing portfolio
- running records
- notes from small group instruction

Using information from these assessments, they create a thorough picture of each child's progress as a reader and writer during that grading period.

Summary of Phonics Assessment

The assessment tools described in this chapter are not simply tasks teachers complete and file away. In contrast, they are intricately woven into the fabric of each day so that distinctions between assessment and instruction are often blurred to the point of invisibility. In an efficient and effective manner, teachers select the appropriate assessment tools to:

- Learn about students' phonics understandings.
- Provide direction for future lessons to support learning.
- Engage children in reading and writing.
- Provide instruction specific to each student's increasing knowledge of letters, sounds, and words.

3

Help for Children Who Struggle with Phonics

Excellent instruction is the best intervention for children who demonstrate problems learning to read. (Snow et al., 1998, p. 3)

Although the school year is almost half over, JoEllen does not yet understand the concept of word and has not been able to independently represent the sounds she hears in words. She is hesitant to try. Mrs. Hootman has chosen the one-on-one focus of a writing conference to assist JoEllen with her writing. Step by step she asks questions and provides the thinking that JoEllen needs to be successful. At the end of the conference she summarizes the process. We join their conference in progress. Mrs. Hootman is assisting JoEllen to write the words *little kittens*. JoEllen has written *cateles* to represent those two words.

MRS. HOOTMAN: (Covers *cateles* with correction tape and draws two lines on the tape, indicating two words are to be written.) What letter does *little* begin with?

JOELLEN: *L* (writes an *L*)

MRS. HOOTMAN: What other letters do you hear?

JOELLEN: My mom tried to teach me. I don't remember.

MRS. HOOTMAN: The next letter is the vowel *I*.

JoEllen writes *I*.

MRS. HOOTMAN: What do you hear in the middle of *little*?

JOELLEN: *T* (writes *T*)

MRS. HOOTMAN: What do you hear at the end [of the word]?

JOELLEN says the word *little* and shrugs.

MRS. HOOTMAN: Say it again and listen to the end.

JOELLEN: *T*? I'm not sure.

MRS. HOOTMAN: (Nods to indicate *T* is the right answer.) There are two *T*'s in the middle, so write another *T* down.

JoEllen writes another *T*.

MRS. HOOTMAN: There is another sound at the end: *littLe*.

JOELLEN: *L*

MRS. HOOTMAN: There is another *L*.

JoEllen writes it down.

MRS. HOOTMAN: Let's try *kittens*.

JoEllen writes *C*.

MRS. HOOTMAN: Two letters make the same sound. It is *K*. (She covers the *C* with correction tape.) Let's do a *K*.

JoEllen writes *K*.

MRS. HOOTMAN: What other letters do you hear?

JoEllen shrugs.

MRS. HOOTMAN: I'm going to write the middle. (She writes *itte*.) What do you hear at the end of *kitteN*?

JoEllen shrugs.

MRS. HOOTMAN: Say *kitten*. What do you hear at the end?

JOELLEN: *kitten, T*.

MRS. HOOTMAN: I hear *T* in the middle. It would be an *N* at the end. (She writes *N* and reads the word.) *Kitten*. Do you want *kitten* or *kittens*?

JOELLEN: *kittens*.

MRS. HOOTMAN: What letter do we need to add at the end?

JOELLEN: *K*? *T*? *A*?

MRS. HOOTMAN: It's like the sound in *birdS*, and *dogS*. What letter is it?

JoEllen shrugs.

MRS. HOOTMAN: It's *S* we hear at the end of all those words. (She reads aloud the text thus far.) *The three little kittens.* What else do you want to say?

(The conference continues in this way creating two more sentences. Then Mrs. Hootman asks JoEllen to read the text they have created together. JoEllen reads it successfully.)

MRS. HOOTMAN: Good job reading. Do the same things when you are alone. Say the words and hear the letters and write them down and leave spaces between the words.

DECISION: Guide the student through the writing process slowly in very small steps being sure the child is attending to the task. Don't accept an excuse or a shrug as a reason to stop.

When teachers like Mrs. Hootman believe all children can learn to read and write, they accept responsibility to help all children move forward in their literacy learning. They attempt to do whatever it takes to reach every student. They understand that children come to school with different preparations—background knowledge, language experiences, interests, and abilities—and they respect these differences. They agree that children learn to read by reading and to write by writing. They also agree that explicit instruction in the forms of teacher demonstration and modeling of strategies and skills is necessary, some of the time, to enable some children to become successful readers and writers.

This chapter addresses the strugglers. They are the children who experience difficulty with the foundations of literacy—oral language development, print awareness, and phonological awareness. All children come to school having some experience with print during their daily lives; however, the nature and extent of these experiences varies widely. Children's ability to learn phonics is directly related to the frequency and quality of their informal experiences with written and oral language. If children don't come to school with a wide variety of literacy experiences, then teachers must provide those experiences.

The teachers featured in this book think about literacy teaching and learning in similar ways. They understand reading as a complex act that involves orchestration of the language cueing systems—semantic cues (systems of meaning), syntactic cues (knowledge of the structure of language and grammar), graphophonic cues (knowledge of letters and sounds), and pragmatics (social and cultural circumstances that influence language usage) to create meaning. They use an assessment-to-instruction model of teaching. Both formal and informal methods are used to assess learners' strengths and needs. Information from observations, interviews, oral readings, written products, and tests help teachers decide what needs to be taught, how it should be taught, and with whom. Chapter Two on assessment describes informal assessment strategies and standardized instruments that look at children's phonics knowledge.

In this chapter, we look at various ways teachers can reach struggling readers and writers. These are not earth-shaking, revolutionary ideas. As suggested by the opening quote for this chapter, the strugglers do not necessarily need different instruction, but they do need high-quality instruction. These are the children who, for whatever reasons, are not figuring it out. They need a teacher prepared to reach out to them. Since teachers attempt to offer excellent instruction to all their students, how will this teaching vary for the strugglers? We will discuss several ways to plan and interact to improve instruction.

- Group students thoughtfully for instruction.
- Establish and maintain a mutual focus.
- Assist student performance.
- Encourage student self-regulation.
- Promote phonemic awareness.

We will also share teacher problem solving. An extended chart at the end of the chapter focuses on phonics instruction, describing teacher thinking, decisions, and examples of possible teacher talk based on observations of learners.

The teaching we explain and illustrate provides literacy instruction in a meaning-centered way. To assist children's sense making, teachers use repeated demonstrations or modeling of reading and writing for different purposes and audiences. Demonstrations move at a slow pace to include think alouds or explicit talk about text structures, letter-sound knowledge, punctuation, and spelling to make clear what good readers do to get to the meaning of the text. This process of assisting children's construction of understanding is present in whole group, small group, and one-on-one teaching situations.

Grouping

When children come to school with very different levels of phonics ability, it is obvious they do not all need the same instruction. For example, a first-grade boy reading at the third-grade level will not benefit from the same phonics instruction as the boy sitting next to him who is not yet able to hear the individual sounds in words. When teachers individualize, they plan and teach with each child in mind instead of thinking of their students as a homogenous group of learners who all need the same thing at the same time. Teachers think about their students' varying abilities when they plan lessons and decide groupings. Which students need instruction in particular phonics skills and strategies? Individualized instruction does not mean all teaching is done one-on-one. In any size group, teachers individualize the instruction by asking focused questions based on each student's abilities and needs. Thus, the key to reaching all students in any size group is knowledge of what each student already knows and what that student is currently trying to learn.

Whole Group

Phonics instruction can occur in whole group settings such as read alouds, shared reading, or interactive reading. In the whole group setting, teachers can individualize instruction through management of who participates. How do teachers decide which students should have a turn to talk in a large group? Some teachers call on children randomly, perhaps alternating boys and girls. The teacher may use a system that ensures everyone gets a turn, such as going through a stack of 3 × 5 cards with each child's name on a separate card. She may decide to call on both volunteers and nonvolunteers. Sometimes teachers have specific reasons for calling on a particular child to contribute, such as reinforcement, inclusion, and encouragement. Mrs. Abreu at Cline Elementary is particularly skilled at reaching every student during whole group shared and interactive writing. She explains:

> I want to get everybody involved. That's how I keep their attention because they never know when I'm going to call on them to come up and write. Everybody has a role. It's a collaborative writing. I need them [the hesitant children] to be up there [using the pen] to show that they can have success. We're a community and we're working on this together.

When she wants to reinforce previous teaching with a particular child, Mrs. Abreu may ask that child to share. As the child works, he not only indicates what has been learned, but he also gets an opportunity to deepen his understanding by working on putting it in his own words to explain to his classmates. Mrs. Abreu may ask a child to contribute to help the child feel included in the process as a reader and writer. When she wants to provide a successful experience for a student, she asks the child she knows has the necessary information to contribute to the text. Because children often know the letters that represent the sounds in their names before any other letters, teachers may ask children to supply the first letter of their names during teacher-led phonemic segmentation.

Small Group

Teachers may chose to concentrate instruction for certain students by dropping down from whole group instruction to a smaller group of just a few learners. The challenge, or course, is that the rest of the class must be self-directed for a period of time and not need the teacher's direct attention. None of the classrooms described in this book have teacher aides. A few classrooms sometimes have parent volunteers who work with individuals or a group of students.

To make small group work possible, teachers can organize their rooms to facilitate independent work. The students who are not with the teacher may be working with a partner or individually. They may be at assigned or chosen learning stations. They may each have a folder of activities to work on. Children can work on their own if they feel ownership and responsibility for the room. Materials and areas of the room should be labeled. Students need easy access to both materials and clean-up supplies. To help students work independently successfully, teachers invest time in the beginning of the year to train the students to work without direct teacher attention for a portion of each day. Routines and procedures need to be established and practiced. Students need to know when, how, and where to get needed materials, store works under construction, and submit works for teacher attention. To promote independence, children may be encouraged to use other students as resources before asking the teacher. (Teachers say, "Ask three, before you ask me.") Each day before independent work time, the teacher may review the posted rules and work options to remind students of their responsibilities and her expectations.

The reward for the time invested in organizing the room and training students to work independently is the teacher being free to work with a small group of learners. Teachers form these small groups based on the objectives of their lessons and the students' common needs. As the objectives and needs change, the members of the groups change. For example, Mrs. Swanson and Mrs. Hootman try to conduct several guided reading sessions daily with three to five children in each group. They include the strugglers in these groups more often to provide more support and monitor their phonics progress more closely.

In the following excerpt, the guided reading group of three children is going to read *The Biggest Cake in the World* (Cowley, 1988). They discuss cake-baking experiences and flip through the book before they read. Mrs. Swanson helps the children learn to attend to letters and sounds.

MRS. SWANSON: O.K. And on this page you can see she has a saw. A special kind of saw. It has a chain. If you were reading the word *chain*, what would you expect at the beginning of the word?

(The students scan the words on the page.)

JOEY: I'd say *sh*.

MRS. SWANSON: How about you two [other students]?

MIKE: *C, H*

FRED: *C, H*

MRS. SWANSON: Some of you say *S, H* and some say *C, H*. Which is it? Like *cheese, chainsaw*, or *chocolate*.

JOEY: *C, H*

Mrs. Swanson nods, confirming Joey's answer.

Mrs. Swanson is scaffolding the boys' learning through careful questioning. She guides them in the use of analogy, asking them to apply the sound-letter relationships from known words to a new word.

DECISION: Since *chain* will probably be an unfamiliar word to these students, remind them to use the sound-to-letter relationships they know so they can cross-check sounds with visual information to figure out unknown words.

Individual Work

A teacher may decide to work one-on-one with a student. This instruction offers the unique opportunity of total concentration on one learner. No child is neglected if each one has a turn to work individually with the teacher on a regular basis. Some teachers reach the strugglers through individual reading conferences. Mrs. Orlich daily conducts individual reading conferences with her lower progress readers during the language arts block. As the other children read independently, she calls children to her desk to read aloud. Mrs. Orlich provides skill and strategy instruction focusing on the meaning of the story and how to figure out words or rethink miscues. She keeps track of what is taught and makes notations about reading progress. We include an example of her work during a conference with Paul, a reader who has difficulty connecting the letter-sound relations he knows with actual reading in books. Here we see him struggling with the word *with*.

MRS. ORLICH: What does *W* say?

PAUL: *w-a*

MRS. ORLICH: (pointing to the *I*) What is this letter? What does it say here?

PAUL: *w-i* (long *I* sound)

MRS. ORLICH: (Rereads the phrase to provide context.) *Mom helps Dad wi* (makes short *I* sound).

PAUL: *w-i* (repeats the short *I* sound used by Mrs. Orlich).

MRS. ORLICH: Now *T* and *H* together. *Th* (shows *th* with her tongue between her teeth). *Wi-th.*

PAUL: *with.* (He then continues reading.)

Mrs. Orlich makes the notation *Review vowels and th* on Paul's reading progress chart in the three-ring binder. (The page provides spaces for the date, book level, observation, and instruction provided.)

In this example, we see Mrs. Orlich model a strategy and work with Paul on the noted skills. She uses kinesthetic cues to reinforce the sound of the *TH* digraph.

> **DECISION**: Demonstrate rereading the sentence for context to support Paul's attempts at figuring out unknown words.

Individual writing conferences are common in the classrooms in this book. Sometimes they are quick exchanges where the teacher circulates among the students. Other times they are extended lessons where the teacher invests a longer period of time (five to ten minutes) moving the literacy learning of one child forward. In the following example, the students are each creating a page for a class book about Christmas dreams. The writing prompt is to describe what (instead of sugarplums) is dancing in your head when you go to bed before Christmas. Mrs. Moore walks around the room and observes the children. In a half hour, she works with eleven different students for a total of fifteen conferences. She returns to the strugglers several times to check on their progress and provide assistance. The following dialogue represents her work with Kevin during their two conferences. She works with him to get him started, leaves him to work independently and returns to check on his progress.

MRS. MOORE: What do you want [to receive for Christmas]?

KEVIN: A fire truck. (He has the letter *f* on his paper.)

MRS. MOORE: You have the first letter. What ones come next?

Kevin looks at the teacher but does not talk.

MRS. MOORE: Listen. Watch me. (She points to her mouth, slowly
     pronounces whole words, emphasizing *I* sound.) *f-I-r-e*.

KEVIN: *R*

MRS. MOORE: There is an *R*, but there is a vowel first. *fIre*.

KEVIN: *A*

MRS. MOORE: That would be *fAre*. What is the vowel?

KEVIN: *I*

MRS. MOORE: Good. (Kevin writes *I* on the paper. Mrs. Moore points to
     the paper.) Now the *R*. (Kevin writes the *R*.) Then a silent letter.

KEVIN: *E* (He writes the *E*.)

MRS. MOORE: (She nods.) Good, now *truck*. How does it start?

They segment the sounds of the word in a similar way with Kevin writing letters. They discuss the vowel sound. At the end of their first conference, he has written *tr c*.

Mrs. Moore moves on to another student, leaving him to work independently. After eleven other quick conferences, she returns to Kevin. He has not written anything since she worked with him earlier. She resumes work on the vowel sound in *truck*.

MRS. MOORE: What do you hear? *u* like *umbrella*.

KEVIN: *U*

Mrs. Moore nods.

Kevin writes the *U*.

MRS. MOORE: You have the *C* (points to his paper), but you need more
     [letters].

KEVIN: *K*

She nods and he tries to write the *K* between the *U* and the *C* on his
     paper.

MRS. MOORE: (Places her hand on his hand to stop his writing.) It goes
     at the end after the *C*.

Kevin writes the *K* at the end of the word.

MRS. MOORE: What did you write? (She points to the paper.)

KEVIN: *Truck.*

MRS. MOORE: *Fire truck.* If you put them together they make one word.

> **DECISION**: Support Kevin's left-to-right phonemic segmentation of a word by providing pronunciation with emphasis on the next part to be written, and by confirming correct attempts to write the sounds he hears.

In our study of phonics instruction, we have documented many extended writing conferences that focused on children's encoding problems. See Chapter Nine for examples and detailed information about this kind of individualized instruction.

Concentration of Instruction

Struggling readers and writers need to be drawn into learning and given extensive scaffolding. We think of scaffolding as a support system of teacher questions and comments that direct the child's attention and facilitate learning. In any whole group activity, the challenge is to reach all students successfully. For some activities, teachers find it more effective to work with small groups. This format offers the advantage of a closer match of materials and instruction to fit each student's needs. Simply based on a smaller number of students, it is possible for the teacher to encourage each child to participate, watch each child more closely, and supply the information or strategy each child needs to be successful. Instruction is concentrated in smaller groups in two ways: a more consistent mutual focus and more individualized scaffolding.

Mutual Focus

Having a mutual focus means two people establish and maintain shared attention on the work at hand. Teachers agree that attention is a prerequisite for learning. The possibility of both the teacher and the student closely attending to each other is less likely in a whole group setting. The larger the group, the less accountable each child may feel toward participating in the learning activity and the more distractions there may be. Although teachers try to gain and hold everyone's attention all the time, it may not be easy with a large group of young students. Teachers understand that not all quiet students looking at them are listening. What about the ones who are obviously not listening, or not looking, or not holding still long enough to either look or listen? When starting work with a large group, Mrs. Abreu often says something similar to the following:

Now, everybody's on their bottoms. And, I want you to look at me. I want you to look me right in the eye. I need you to listen to Mrs. Abreu. You have ideas. I know this is hard, but on the 156th day of school, you should be able to work hard. I want everyone to help read this.

Mutual focus is a two-way process. The child needs to pay attention to the teacher and the teacher pays attention to the child. The more children in the group, the more challenging it is for one teacher to monitor all students simultaneously. As the size of the group decreases, the instruction becomes more concentrated because the teacher's attention is less diluted. In one-on-one instruction, the teacher and learner can continually adjust to each other to keep their mutual focus of attention on the literacy learning. When both people are attending, the teaching and learning dialogue can begin.

WAYS TO CAPTURE AND MAINTAIN STUDENTS' FOCUS

Alter voice pitch or volume

Move around the room

Make eye contact

Ask for "every eye here"

Request students to "think with me now"

Point to words

Stop and wait

Use a child's name

Ask the child to participate

Guide the child's finger(s) to frame or point to a word

Assisted Performance

Struggling readers and writers need thoughtful help. The closer a teacher monitors a child, the better she can accommodate him with appropriate instruction. Sensitive scaffolding of a child's learning is based on knowing what the student has already learned, what the child is capable of learning with help, and what is currently beyond the child's reach, even with help. There is no point teaching what the child has already learned and has under control. That leads to boredom. Equally, there is no point teaching material beyond the child's current assisted reach. That leads to frustration.

Some children need minimal assisted performance. They can observe someone else doing something and figure out how to do it on their own. Most children benefit from some assisted performance. The strugglers need a great deal of assisted performance. They need someone to do it with them; most likely more than once; most likely over and over again. (JoEllen in the opening vignette of this chapter is an example.) During assisted performance, the teacher and learners develop an understanding of *terms*: What does the teacher mean when she says, "Sound it out"? and *actions*: What does the teacher want when she says, "Use your finger"? to work together with text. Whether reading or writing, the teacher provides whatever is needed to help the child be successful. Together they fill the gap between what the child is able to do and what the chosen reading or writing activity requires.

During assisted performance, the teacher aims to gradually contribute an increasingly smaller percentage of the work as the child assumes an increasingly larger portion of the process. In the beginning, the teacher may have to do all the work, or the vast majority of it, and the child observes and/or contributes minimally. At first the teacher regulates the child by providing much of the thinking. Over time, the child can do more and more. The following is an example of a student who gradually moves forward over time. The two conferences provide a way to contrast what the child is able to contribute to the writing process. In the first conference, we see Tammy is at the very early levels of writing development. She writes random letters to represent the meaning she constructs as she imagines her text.

TAMMY: It's about me and my sister.

MRS. EDDEY: Now what about you and your sister?

TAMMY: Me and my sister at the park.

MRS. EDDEY: What did you do at the park?

TAMMY: We played in the swing set. We played in the sand.

MRS. EDDEY: What words are you going to put down on this piece of paper?

TAMMY: About that.

MRS. EDDEY: Now let's work on the thing. *Me, m-e* (emphasizing the sounds). What does *me* start with?

The conference continues as Mrs. Eddey segments the sounds and Tammy identifies the appropriate letters for each one.

> **DECISION**: Assist Tammy's performance by attempting to establish a definite text and show how to represent it with appropriate letters.

This kind of letter-sound support continued in individual conferences during writing workshop time. By mid-January, Tammy was segmenting words successfully but struggling to identify which vowel to write. In this second conference, Tammy is attempting to write *We did all of our home-work.* She has some letters on the page. This day's whole group instruction included minilessons focusing on vowel sounds.

MRS. EDDEY: (Seeing the *D* for *did*, she talks about the vowel sound in the word.) We talked about this [vowel] today. (She makes the short *I* sound.) Say the sound. What letter makes that sound? *d-i.*

Tammy makes short *I* sound.

MRS. EDDEY: So each time you hear the short *I* sound in your word, what letter are you going to write, Tammy?

TAMMY: *I*

The conference continues as they work on *our* and *homework*. At the end of the conference Tammy decides on a new sentence to add (*We woke up in the morning*). They talk about how Tammy can work on that sentence independently.

DECISION: Assist Tammy's performance by connecting her writing with the day's vowel lesson.

These two conferences show a shift in instruction. In a little over a month, the child is able to contribute a larger portion of the writing work. In response, the teacher modifies her questions and contributes less. In the earlier conference, the teacher is pronouncing all the words slowly as the child listens for sounds she knows and identifies appropriate letters. In the later conference, the child has been able to write down appropriate letters for initial consonants by herself, so the teacher focuses on helping her hear and record the vowel sounds.

Read alouds and write alouds are examples of literacy activities that depend heavily on teacher regulation. They invite children into the world of readers and writers, but the children participate more as observers. The teacher provides the majority of the work and thinking involved. During shared or interactive reading and writing, the teacher demonstrates and models, requesting and incorporating students' help to build the bridge. Guided reading and also guided writing require a shift in ownership for the literacy work from the teacher to the children. The end goal is for the children to be able to do the work and thinking of independent reading and writing.

Self-Regulation

The teacher's ultimate objective is for students to become independent, self-regulated readers and writers. How do we help children to regulate themselves? Two processes are involved: routines and self-monitoring.

Routines are a sequence of steps that becomes automatic through repetition. Initially, the teacher provides the structure for going about a literacy task. The teacher repeats the same sequence of steps over the school year, often using the exact same language. This systematic talk is the way the teacher shares her thinking with the child. By thinking aloud, she demonstrates how readers and writers work through different literacy tasks. Chapter Nine on whole group writing provides a description of teacher demonstrations that shows how teachers can describe their thinking and decisions.

The teacher shares the strategies that work for her and have worked for other students. At first she explains ways to think about working through the task involved in reading and writing. Gradually the child adopts the teacher's talk. The teacher still needs to guide the process, often by asking questions that serve as verbal prompts of what needs to be done next. During the conference in the opening vignette, Mrs. Hootman supported JoEllen's sound and letter matching by asking a series of questions such as: What is the first word? What does it start with? What's the next letter? What other letters do you hear? What do you hear at the end? Before each writing task, the teachers always review basic phonics strategies. The following assignment involves illustrating and labeling characters from the nursery rhyme "Hey, Diddle, Diddle."

MRS. HOOTMAN: How can you label your pictures? What can you do if you go to write *fiddle* and you think, "Ooo, I don't know how to spell *fiddle*?" What can you do when you go to label that [drawing of a] fiddle? Ned?

NED: Spell it.

MRS. HOOTMAN: How can you think of how to label *fiddle* if you are not sure how to spell it?

JOSIE: Sound it out

MRS. HOOTMAN: Right. Sound it out. Say: *f-i-d-l*. You can say it out loud: *fiddle*. You can say, "Oh! I hear an *F* at the beginning of that" and just write the letters that you hear. You could ask a friend. You can look up here at the chart and try to find *fiddle*. You could look at the book. So there are lots of different things you can do to try to figure that out.

> **DECISION**: Review the list of strategies for writing a word you don't know how to spell by asking the children to share the strategies they remember, then supply several more.

Over time, the teacher's language becomes the child's thinking. The teacher then begins to ask the child to share his thinking—to bring to a level of awareness how he went about attacking and accomplishing a task. This is the way the teacher monitors the child's thinking and demonstrates what the child should be doing for himself. In the following example from a guided reading group, after they have read the book, Mrs. Swanson asks the students to explain why they self-corrected their first attempt at a word from *salt* (which was incorrect) to *sugar* (which was correct).

MRS. SWANSON: On page four you said, "She had a trailer of *salt.*" You changed that to *sugar.* Why?

No student responds.

MRS. SWANSON: Put your finger under it [the word].

MIKE: *S*

MRS. SWANSON: Yes, it starts with *S.* Why did you change what you read?

PETE: *Salt* has *S, A; sugar* had *S, U.*

Mrs. Swanson nods to confirm Pete's answer.

> **DECISION**: Ask children to explain their use of strategies to help them realize how they self-corrected using visual information and to help other group members learn how it can be done.

The final step is for the children to take over the job of self-monitoring by continually asking themselves if what they are reading or writing is making sense without being prompted by the teacher.

A recognizable pattern occurring in these classrooms is *I do it* (the teacher demonstrates a process or strategy), *We do it* (the teacher and children collaborate using the process or strategy), and *You do it* (the child works with the process or strategy independently). These teachers spend a great deal of time with the strugglers in the middle step, *We do it,* demonstrating, thinking aloud, and sharing how to monitor reading and writing for sense making. The teacher provides a framework for learning. At first, the teacher's comments provide thinking for the problem. Responsibility gradually shifts from teacher to student as the child starts to provide the oral language and thinking. Finally, the child has made that learning a part of his knowledge and can do it independently.

Phonemic Awareness

Aware that struggling readers often lack phonemic awareness, teachers lead children to attend to the phonological aspects of speech, and, ultimately, to help them hear the phonemes in words. Activities such as reading aloud and shared reading from quality children's literature support children's learning through the use of rhyme and alliteration. Poetry can be used to help develop phonological awareness. With the poem displayed on large chart paper, children read the poem together and discuss the discovery of patterns within the text. (See Chapter Seven on children's literature and Chapter Five on word study for examples of teachers using books and poetry effectively to develop phonological awareness.)

Whole group and individual writing are pervasive in the classrooms in this book. As the teacher and children write together, they systematically work on the sound structure of words, stretching out (or segmenting) words to listen carefully for the individual sounds across spoken words. Every morning at Grayhill school, Mrs. Moore and her whole class write The Daily News. The children supply the thoughts and the teacher writes on a large sheet of lined paper attached to the chalkboard with heavy magnets. Mrs. Moore says the words slowly and carefully so children can hear the sounds in the words. She emphasizes the phoneme they are currently trying to find letters to represent. The children answer together. In the following excerpt, they are working on the word *valentine's*.

MRS. MOORE: *Valentine's Day* (repeating the part of the sentence not yet written). It is a special day. (She hints that it will begin with a capital letter.)

STUDENTS: Capital *V*. (Mrs. Moore writes it down.)

MRS. MOORE: All right, listen *v-A-l*

STUDENTS: *A*

MRS. MOORE: *A* (She writes it.) *v-a-L*

STUDENTS: *L* (Mrs. Moore writes it down.)

MRS. MOORE: *en*

STUDENTS: *N*

MRS. MOORE: *E, N* (She writes it.) *tine*

STUDENTS: *T, I* (A few students offer other letters.)

MRS. MOORE: O.K. Spell it.

STUDENTS: *T, I*

MRS. MOORE: *T, I* . . . What else?

Students respond, some saying *L* and some saying *M*.

MRS. MOORE: *M? valentiN?*

No student responds.

MRS. MOORE: (She writes down *N*.) What's next? What do I need at the end? This letter makes the *I* long.

STUDENTS: *E* [quietly]

MRS. MOORE: I didn't hear you.

STUDENTS: *E* [loudly]

MRS. MOORE: *E* (She writes it down and rereads the sentence thus far.) *On Friday it will be Valentine's* (She writes *S* as she finishes pronouncing the word.)

> **DECISION**: Use the whole group shared writing setting to demonstrate how to listen and record the sounds in words by pronouncing the words and asking questions.

Games can support phonological awareness by requiring students to isolate or segment one or more of the phonemes of a spoken word, to blend or combine a sequence of separate phonemes into a word, or to manipulate the phonemes within a word (adding, subtracting, or rearranging phonemes of one word to make a different word). For example, children with phonemic awareness are able to discern that *camp* and *soap* end with the same sound; that *blood* and *brown* begin with the same sound; or, more advanced still, that removing the *M* from *smell* results in *sell.* For some children, these language activities are much easier than for others. See Chapter Five on word study for suggestions of useful tongue twisters, riddles, and activities.

Observations and Decisions

Teachers learn a great deal by watching and listening to their students. They think about why the strugglers behave in the ways they do. They ask themselves questions. They make decisions and try an approach. They then watch and listen to decide what to do next. The following table shares this process for children who are not learning phonics. They are grouped into four sets of teacher observations:

- The child does not respond or makes minimal attempts to read or write.
- The child does not focus on the text.
- The child demonstrates he understand the basic parts of the reading and writing process, but has not put it all together.
- The child demonstrates that she does not understand the basic parts of the reading and writing process.

Each section lists in the left column several questions a teacher may ask herself followed by decisions of possible things to try. The right column offers a few examples of things a teacher might say to a child and/or his family.

TABLE 3-1   Guiding Struggling Readers and Writers

TEACHER OBSERVATION: THE CHILD DOES NOT RESPOND OR MAKES MINIMAL ATTEMPTS TO READ OR WRITE

Teacher Thinking and Decisions

1. Is he waiting for me to do it for him?
   - Wait and listen.
   - Smile and use an encouraging facial expression.
   - Give him ample time to complete the tasks and be successful. He will learn that I am not going to supply the information and/or answer if I know he can do it.

2. Does he think he can't do it?
   - Convey the belief he can succeed.
   - Remind him of other things he has worked at and been successful.
   - Point out things he does know and can use.
   - Start with the area of strength. If he is stronger in writing, use it to practice reading, and vice versa.
   - Read a version of *The Little Engine That Could*.

3. Is he unwilling to do the necessary hard work?
   - Recognize the effort involved.
   - Share the belief that the benefits are substantial.
   - Provide a real audience for his work.

4. Is he afraid to take a risk? Is he a perfectionist who does not want to be wrong?
   - Let him know I expect he will make mistakes.
   - Recognize the effort and thinking that caused him to make a miscue.
   - Encourage him to verbalize his thinking so I can know how to help him.
   - Prompt him by asking questions to guide his thinking.
   - Confirm and celebrate when he does respond.
   - Praise any and all success.
   - Demonstrate having difficulties during a minilesson and talk about how to problem solve.

TEACHER OBSERVATION: THE CHILD DOES NOT RESPOND OR MAKES MINIMAL ATTEMPTS TO READ OR WRITE

Examples of Teacher Talk

"I'll wait for you to figure it out."

"What strategies could you use here?"

"Where will you begin?"

"I can't help you until you try something."

"Remember when we did this as a group?"

"Tell me what you think you might try."

"You can do this. We will just take it slowly."

"I know you know the sound for the letter that starts this word because it also starts your name."

"I'll begin this word if you will finish it."

"Remember how hard you worked on that card for your mother and how well it turned out?"

"I know learning to read and write is hard work, but it is worth it. You can learn about interesting things and have fun, too."

"How can I make this easier for you?"

"Why don't you write a letter to your brother in the Army?"

"We all find words that we don't know when we are reading. We try to figure them out and make our best guess."

"Good guess! That word could be *Bill* because it starts with a *B*, but it is not. Try again."

"Let me hear what you are trying to figure out."

"Right. That's what readers and writers do, go back and read what they wrote."

"What do readers (or writers) do next?"

"Thank you for taking a risk."

TABLE 3-1   (cont.)

TEACHER OBSERVATION: THE CHILD DOES NOT RESPOND OR MAKES MINIMAL ATTEMPTS TO READ OR WRITE

Teacher Thinking and Decisions

5. Is he not interested? Does he see no use for literacy in his life?
   - Share enthusiasm for literacy.
   - Ask students to develop a list of reasons why we need to learn to read.
   - Do real reading for real purposes. (Bring in a cereal box offer or contest that would interest him.)
   - Use his interests for literacy choices.
   - Publish the child's writing.
   - Give him a chance in the reader's chair and author's chair to share what he has read and written with his friends.
   - Send books home.
   - Suggest a half-hour nightly family reading time.
   - Recommend books for the family to get at the library.
   - Take him to get a library card.
   - Show parents how to work with him effectively.

TEACHER OBSERVATION: THE CHILD DOES NOT FOCUS ON THE TEXT

Teacher Thinking and Decisions

1. Do other things distract the child?
   - Work with her in a small group or individually.
   - Ask her to put distracting objects out of view.
   - Cue her verbally or nonverbally to attend.
   - Use a finger or other pointer to indicate words as reading.
   - Offer a secluded spot, such as a reading cubby, study nook, or dividing wall to screen out distractions.
   - Try a different type of instruction.

TEACHER OBSERVATION: THE CHILD DOES NOT RESPOND OR MAKES MINIMAL ATTEMPTS TO READ OR WRITE

Examples of Teacher Talk

"I like reading this joke book. It makes me laugh out loud . . ."

"I'm going to share a letter we received from a former classmate."

"You may chose three books for buddy reading from anywhere in the room."

"If you are ready for a new writing topic today, remember your interests list pasted in the front cover of your journal notebook."

"That's a great question! Where could you find the answer?"

"I know you like cars. Let's find a book about that."

"Who would you like to work with?"

TEACHER OBSERVATION: THE CHILD DOES NOT FOCUS ON THE TEXT

Examples of Teacher Talk

"I only want to see your paper, pencil, and book on your desk right now."

"You need to put all the toys you brought for recess in the basket by the door."

"Clear off your desk."

"Is there a better place for you to sit?"

"Look with me at this large chart."

TABLE 3-1   (cont.)

TEACHER OBSERVATION: THE CHILD DOES NOT FOCUS ON THE TEXT

Teacher Thinking and Decisions

2. Does she come to school troubled?
   - Describe difficulties and ask family for suggestions.
   - Offer help.
   - Take parents to workshops.
   - Give the child a private opportunity to say what is on her mind.
   - Read stories about children in crises.

3. Is she most interested in the social aspects of school?
   - Make use of interest in peers to spark interest in literacy.
   - Encourage her to write a note to a friend.
   - Tell her to read her writing aloud to a work partner right after she writes it (before she forgets what she wrote).
   - Use buddy reading (peers and older students).
   - Use literature circles.
   - Show interest in what she does out of class.

4. Is she not paying attention to the important details?
   - Instruct explicitly on fine points.
   - Use color transparencies or highlight tape to assist focus.
   - Check vision and hearing.

TEACHER OBSERVATION: THE CHILD DEMONSTRATES HE UNDERSTANDS THE BASIC PARTS OF THE READING AND WRITING PROCESS, BUT HAS NOT PUT IT ALL TOGETHER

Teacher Thinking and Decisions

1. What connections doesn't he see?
   - Point out links between the known and unknown (analogy).
   - Work on patterns: word families, word chunks, rhyming words, word sorts, etc.
   - Think out loud when demonstrating reading or writing.
   - Talk about the things good writers and readers do.

TEACHER OBSERVATION: THE CHILD DOES NOT FOCUS ON THE TEXT

Examples of Teacher Talk

"Susan can't stay focused on her schoolwork. How can I help?"
"Is there anything unusual going on at home?"
"Is there something you want to talk about?"
"Are you noticing Susan having problems at home?"

"I noticed you and Alissa play ball together almost every day. Would you like to write a note to her and put it in her mailbox?"
"When you are finished with your writing today, please read it to your work partner to be sure you have it the way you want it."
"Remember to help out your buddy."

"You need to pay attention to which side of the circle you draw the stick on this letter. It makes a big difference because if you put it on the other side, it will be a different letter with a different sound. . . ."

TEACHER OBSERVATION: THE CHILD DEMONSTRATES HE UNDERSTANDS THE BASIC PARTS OF THE READING AND WRITING PROCESS, BUT HAS NOT PUT IT ALL TOGETHER

Examples of Teacher Talk

"If you know the letter that starts the word *ball* or *boy*, then you know the letter to start the word *batter*."
"When I am writing the word *success*, I think about the cheer we do at football games and I remember how to spell it."
"When readers get stuck on a word sometimes they go back to the beginning of the sentence and read it again and think about what word would make sense there."

TABLE 3-1   (cont.)

TEACHER OBSERVATION: THE CHILD DEMONSTRATES HE UNDERSTANDS THE BASIC PARTS OF THE READING AND WRITING PROCESS, BUT HAS NOT PUT IT ALL TOGETHER

Teacher Thinking and Decisions

- Ask the child to verbalize thinking so I can find out what connections are being made and build on them.
- Demonstrate making connections in shared reading and writing.

2. Do I need to teach this again or differently?
   - Say it over and over again.
   - Think of different ways to say the same thing.
   - Ask a peer to explain it.

3. What does he know that he isn't using?
   - Remind him of strategies, sounds, letters, and conventions of print that he does know that are useful in this situation.
   - Encourage use of the classroom: word wall, print on display, books, etc.
   - Ask him to articulate thinking to bring it to a level of consciousness.

4. Is he self-monitoring?
   - Prompt him to continually listen to himself read, and to read what he wrote.
   - Encourage him to crosscheck his attempts with all cueing systems.
   - Tape-record the child and have him listen to himself read.

TEACHER OBSERVATION: THE CHILD DEMONSTRATES THAT SHE DOES NOT UNDERSTAND THE BASIC PARTS OF THE READING AND WRITING PROCESS

Teacher Thinking and Decisions

1. Does she know the conventions of print?
   - Talk about letters, words, and spaces between them.
   - Demonstrate how to handle a book.

TEACHER OBSERVATION: THE CHILD DEMONSTRATES HE UNDERSTANDS THE BASIC PARTS OF THE READING AND WRITING PROCESS, BUT HAS NOT PUT IT ALL TOGETHER

Examples of Teacher Talk

"Do you know a word that looks (or sounds) like this one?"

"You know _____."

"What made you say that?"

"Last week we talked about rhyming words. Today we are going to look at word families."

"Who can explain this to Bruce in a different way?"

"What part of this don't you understand?"

"What can you do to check that guess?"

"Where can you find that word in this room?"

"How did you decide *C* was the right letter to start writing *color*?"

"Does that make sense?

"Does that look right?"

"Does that sound right?"

"You read *happy*. If the word was *happy*, what letter would you expect to see at the beginning of the word?"

TEACHER OBSERVATION: THE CHILD DEMONSTRATES THAT SHE DOES NOT UNDERSTAND THE BASIC PARTS OF THE READING AND WRITING PROCESS

Examples of Teacher Talk

"Remember to start at the top of the page."

"It is hard to read writing with no spaces between the words because you can't see where one word ends and the next begins."

TABLE 3-1   (cont.)

TEACHER OBSERVATION: THE CHILD DEMONSTRATES THAT SHE DOES NOT UNDERSTAND THE BASIC PARTS OF THE READING AND WRITING PROCESS
Teacher Thinking and Decisions
• Tell how the eyes move to read. Track with a pointer or a finger.

2. Is she unable to hear the sounds in words?
  • Use predictable text with rhyme, rhythm, and repetition (read poetry, recite/chant, sing).
  • Stretch words out to hear the individual sounds (phonemes).

3. Does she not understand the alphabetic system?
  • Demonstrate what we say can be written down using certain letters to represent certain sounds.
  • Serve as a scribe for a story she dictates.
  • Teach letter-sound combinations through cards, games, cutting letters from magazines, creating *ABC* books, etc.

Conclusion

Teachers create a literate environment with a variety of materials, including children's literature, big books, and class-created stories to interest the strugglers in working with text. They show children that reading and writing are connected to each other and that phonics skills and strategies are an important part of learning how to do both. They provide repetition by continually providing opportunities for reading and writing in various formats so the strugglers can work on the basic phonics concepts repeatedly. The struggling students need many chances to learn skills and practice strategies. The following guidelines support planning for excellent instruction.

TEACHER OBSERVATION: THE CHILD DEMONSTRATES THAT SHE DOES NOT UNDERSTAND THE BASIC PARTS OF THE READING AND WRITING PROCESS

Examples of Teacher Talk

"Let me read it the way you wrote it."

"When you write, put your finger on the paper after each word. Then write the next word on the other side of your finger to make a space between words."

"We start here on the page and read what is at the top first, then go down to the next lower part."

"When we read we start on the left side of the page and read to the right, then go down to the next line and read left to right again."

"Follow the pointer to see what order I am reading these words."

"When I want to write a word I don't know how to spell, I say the word out loud slowly and listen carefully for letter sounds I know."

"Do you know a word that begins like this one?"

"When I write I use the letters of the alphabet to stand for the sounds in the words."

"What letter makes that sound?"

"You tell me your story and I'll write it down."

"See how many different *G*s you can find and cut out of this magazine for our letter board."

- Adjust the concentration of instruction through various groupings.

- Establish a common focus.

- Teach at the child's cutting edge of learning.

- Use systematic routines for literacy work.

- Work to gradually shift the responsibility for reading and writing to the student.

- Instruct explicitly by thinking aloud while demonstrating effective reader and writer behaviors.

CANDACE MOORE:
TEACHER TO TEACHER

I observe the children in my class as I teach. Many of them catch on to reading and writing and they've got it and they're gone, and then there are others who are really struggling. Perhaps they have medical problems or troubles at home. Sometimes they can't hear the sounds of the letters, or they have a speech problem and can't say the letter sounds. Often I do not know exactly what the problem is, but for some children it doesn't seem to come together easily. I always help the children see how they are doing better than they were before. I want them to know their hard work is paying off.

I do a lot of phonics teaching with the whole class through a minilesson or in the shared writing of The Daily News. Each morning the children sit on the rug in the front of the room and dictate sentences. I write them down. I show them what I want them to do when they write on their own. We discuss letter-sound combinations that are not written just like they sound when you say them. After we have several sentences about the date, weather, and activities of the day, we read it together. Next, we usually play I Spy. I ask the children to search for examples of certain phonics generalizations, such as words with a silent *E* at the end, or words with a blend at the beginning.

All my children work individually at some point in time during the day. I walk around and find out who's doing what and who needs help. I try to work with those that need help one-on-one a little bit more. When I find several children who need special help in one area, such as vowel sounds, I put them in a small, selected group. I'll work more with that group on the things they need. I do minilessons to see if I can get them to understand a little bit better.

I want my students to write in every subject. We do group writing of stories or letters on large chart paper. The children do journaling. Sometimes I give them a sentence starter and sometimes I give them a choice of topic. They write for math and social studies. I try to get them writing something every day. In the beginning of the year, the children want me to spell every single word. I don't want them to think I am their dictionary. I give them clues by over-enunciating the words and asking them what they hear at the beginning, middle, and end of the word. Eventually, they spell the words without my help.

I encourage the children to ask their classmates for help. Many classmates can help them just as well as I can with a word, with a letter, with the sounds, or just reading directions. So I try to encourage them to use their classmates. Let them be little teachers. I may ask them to work with each other. Sometimes two strugglers work well together by helping each other out. Sometimes a struggler will work well with an advanced reader.

The strugglers can get motivated because they realize they want to be better readers, too. They put forth that extra effort to learn.

It takes time, but I work to win my students' confidence. They need to know I am on their side. I need to let these students know it's okay to come to me and ask for help. Little by little, they learn they can trust me. I try to build their confidence by saying things like, "You can do this," "We're just going to take it slow," and "We'll just work on it." I point out the things they know and the things they can do. I try to do what I can with my students. It's like putting money in the bank. All the phonics work gradually keeps adding up until one day, you have a nest egg. They may not be saying anything, but if they're paying attention and listening and making connections, sometime in the future they realize they have it and take off on their own. Overall, I'm pleased with the progress of my children in my classroom.

4

Strategies to Develop Phonics Skills

Phonics skills and strategies work together. Strategies are procedures that serve as ways to use specific skills; they help children connect knowledge of letter-sound patterns to their independent reading and writing by providing specific thinking for children to use. When we listen to teachers talk about strategies, we hear explanations of what to do, descriptions of explicit, procedural knowledge. For example, when a first grader reading on his own pauses before a word he doesn't know, Janice Eddey explains the strategy:

> Here's how to get a word you don't know. Think about the meaning. Look at the first letter of the word and get your mouth ready to say that word. Try to say the word and think about whether it makes sense.

Here she explains the use of semantic cues in combination with letter-sound information and monitoring the outcome for meaning. The strategy is to link semantic and letter-sound cues, then test the outcome in terms of making sense.

Strategy support is often based on familiar information and provides a scaffold to guide the learner. For example, Lisa Dapoz works with Francis, a low-progress student who wants to write the word *craft*. The teacher elongates the word *c-r-a-f-t*. Francis listens and writes *C R A*. Mrs. Dapoz encourages her further, "You almost have the whole word." (She says it slowly and emphasizes the *F* sound). "What's that *ff* sound? Like *fist, fun,* and *Francis*?

Francis responds, "F!"

Some of the time, strategy talk is simply reinforcement. The teacher helps children see their actions as procedures that can be repeated. Linda Orlich, for example, is working with a child in a reading conference. The child corrects a miscue after rereading part of the text. Mrs. Orlich points out that action of rereading and making a correction as a strategy that can be used again. She explains, "When you knew what would make sense [in that sentence], you used your strategy to go back and correct the word." The child looks at the word again in light of that strategy reinforcement and reads on.

While it may seem that these three quick examples are tiny threads of instruction, they represent a powerful support network for young readers when woven repeatedly into the daily reading and writing experiences of the classroom. Consistently, children hear strategies explained and see them repeated and reinforced in the context of their use in reading and writing. They practice them in the classroom and eventually use them on their own. The teacher gradually releases support as learners gain confidence in using strategies independently.

Strategies

In this chapter we present eight strategies that we observed over and over (often in combination with each other) as we studied exemplary first-grade classrooms. They are explanations of procedures involving phonics knowledge that occurred as part of instruction in nearly every classroom visit. These strategies help children work through unknown words and solve the letter-sound problems they encounter. They serve as pathways for applying phonics knowledge. We introduce each strategy and then include examples of various ways the teachers talked about them with children. The first strategy is already familiar.

Strategy 1: Use of Onset and Meaning to Figure Out a Word

In this strategy, children simultaneously use the beginning letters of the particular word with their sense of meaning for the sentence to rapidly identify an unknown word. This strategy includes prompts by the teacher such as the following two options:

- Look at the first letters. How does that word start? Get your mouth ready (to make that sound).
- Look at the way the word begins. Now look at the picture. What word would make sense here?

Children combine their knowledge of language and their grasp of sentence meaning with the onset of a word as a prompt. *Onset* means the consonants before the vowel of a syllable (*str* in *street*). The *rime* part of the word is the vowel and any consonants that come after it (*eet* in *street*) (Moustafa, 1997). Of course, teachers don't use the term "onset" as they talk to first graders. Instead, they urge children to look at the beginning of the word and think about that sound while also keeping sentence meaning in mind. Sometimes children refer to pictures and then say a possible word.

Strategy 2: Sound Out a Word by Elongating Its Sounds

This is a commonly used strategy. It means segmenting the sounds from left to right in order to sound out a word, stretching out the sounds, and producing them in order. It is a procedure that gets the decoding started and ensures that the segmented sounds are all included. The next step is blending sounds to get the word.

We know that some of the time the letter-sound patterns are not simply a left-to-right matter. For example, noticing the *E* at the end of *make* helps a first grader say a long *A* sound and that's a right-to-left matter. Recognizing a familiar word chunk like *–ing* at the end of the word may also not need to be sounded out. Obviously, this sounding-out strategy starting with the left and continuing on across the word is not applicable every time. Appropriate teacher talk for this strategy includes two options:

- Sound it out, start at the beginning, and make each sound.
- Stretch that word out, and say it slowly. Find all the sounds that are there.

The flip side of this strategy occurs in writing, where the elongation strategy means segmenting the phonemes of an intended word and matching appropriate letters to sounds. The child is shown how to match letters to needed sounds and is supported through the encoding process as she writes the word. There are many ways that teachers talk about this strategy and many quick decisions they make while helping children write a word. Often the teacher says the segmented sounds while the child listens and writes the letters. This scaffold enables the left-to-right progress to occur and helps with decisions about which letters to write. Again, we tap the teaching of Janice Eddey for an example:

At the beginning of writing workshop, Cindy, a learner just beginning to produce writing, asks for help.

CINDY: I need help spelling *Cinderella*.

MRS. EDDEY: *s-s*

CINDY: (Recognizes the help has begun.) *S*

MRS. EDDEY: *i-n*

CINDY: *N*

MRS. EDDEY: *der*

CINDY: *D*

MRS. EDDEY: *Cin-der-eLL*

CINDY: *L*

MRS. EDDEY: Now *Cin-der-ell-a*. What are you going to write about Cinderella?

CINDY: (Shrugs, looks at her attempted spelling and starts to develop her writing idea.)

Here the strategic support is very basic, just a scaffold to help some segmenting to occur and guide encoding from left to right. Since the point of this quick conference is enabling the child to begin writing about Cinderella, the talk about *S* and *C*, about hearing vowel sounds in a word, about hearing the *er*, is saved for later when those concepts can be developed clearly.

The goal in this writing program is to move the child toward conventional spellings. Throughout the year, Mrs. Eddey conducts editing conferences where she works on conventional spellings and other editing matters. She supports children's use of this sounding-out strategy in conferences by demanding careful attention to each sound. The teacher talk for this strategy could involve these choices:

- Say the word slowly then write the sounds your hear.
- Listen to the word, say it to yourself, and write letters for the sounds you hear.

Strategy 3: Recheck Writing by Rereading and Monitoring Sounds

There are two strategies that involve checking one's work by going back to look again at how sounds are represented. One strategy relates to writing, the other to reading. In the writing-related strategy, children reread words they've written to see if every sound is represented. They check to see if the word looks right and sounds right. For example, a child in Mrs. Eddey's classroom corrects a first try at spelling *Santa*. He wrote *S A T*, but in the editing conference he changes it so every sound is represented. Editing conferences support this rechecking strategy. With guidance, the expectation is that the child will start using this strategy independently while writing. The teacher talk for this strategy includes these options:

- Recheck your words, look closely at the spellings. Are all the sounds you hear written down?
- When you check your spellings, move your finger under the word while you say it. Are all the sounds you hear written down?

Strategy 4: Use Letter-Sound Information to Rethink a Miscue

The doubling back strategy in reading is just like its counterpart in writing. Children rethink and correct a miscue by using phonics cues to help the reading make sense. A miscue is a reader's unexpected response to a text—a difference between what is printed and what is read. It could include a substitution (*house* for *home*), an omission, insertion, or a combination of these (Wilde, 1997). The point of this strategy is that letter-sound relations are part of rethinking and correcting a miscue. They are part of the information that readers use when meaning breaks down. The teacher talk involved is to direct attention to the miscue and help the learner look closely.

For example, Beth Swanson helps first graders in a guided reading group correct a miscue for the word *WANT* in their story. She asks them to point to the word *WANT* in their book.

MRS. SWANSON: What is this?

ANDY: *Like.*

MRS. SWANSON: That's what you said. Check yourself. What does *like* start with?

ANDY: *L*

MRS. SWANSON: And do you see *L* here?

Andy shakes his head to say no.

MRS. SWANSON: What other letters does *like* have?

ANDY: *K*

MRS. SWANSON: Do you see *K* here?

Andy shakes his head to indicate no.

MRS. SWANSON: You need to check what you see.

Eventually this interaction becomes a routine. The initial reminder to recheck may simply involve the teacher pointing at the word where the miscue occurred and expecting the correction. In Linda Orlich's class, for example, this pointing strategy is a key part of some individual conferences. We look at a conference with Marty, a beginning reader, who often reads inaccurately. Mrs. Orlich is trying to get him to look closely at miscues and recheck his reading. The sentence they are reading is *Lamb had no mother.*

MARTY: (reading slowly) Lamb heard on mother.

MRS. ORLICH: Does that make sense?

MARTY: Lamb heard NO mother.

Mrs. Orlich points to the letters of *had* to focus attention. She keeps her fingers under the word.

MRS. ORLICH: Does that make sense?

MARTY: Lamb HAD no mother.

MRS. ORLICH: Good.

The strategy for Marty is to look again at the word, rethinking it with the letter-sound relations in mind. He knows the sentence has to make sense.

Strategy 5: Use Pattern Knowledge to Figure Out Words

This strategy involves making analogies. For example, if children know the word *fight* they can read *blight* by substituting the initial sound. It also entails using relatively consistent letter-sound relationships and word patterns to figure out new words. As the child works from a known word pattern, he applies information to figure out a new word. He makes the connection between known and unknown. A quick example will clarify.

Dorothy is trying to write, *Time to watch TV.*

MRS. SWANSON: Let's look at this word. (Points to *watch*.) Time to watch. *Ch*. What two letters work together to make that sound? Like in *Chandler* (another student).

DOROTHY: *S H*

MRS. SWANSON: That's really close. That's like *Sharon.* If you had *SH*, it would be *watSH*. You want *watCH* like the harder sound *CH*, like *Chad, Chandler.*

Word patterns and analogies serve as tools children can use to figure out new words. We provide two examples of teacher talk from our observations. The first relates to reading, the second to writing:

- You know the word *feet*, you can figure out this one. That's an *M*. (*meet*)

- What do you hear at the beginning of the word *that*? Do you know how to write *the*? Do *the* and *that* begin the same way? What do you think the letters are? Write the word *that*.

The teacher's strategy guidance in each example focuses on what the child knows about letters, sounds, and word patterns and helps the child connect it to the needed word.

Strategy 6: Kinesthetic Information

Children may be unclear about how specific speech sounds are made and confuse some sounds that have not been sufficiently differentiated from each other. This strategy focuses on the way the mouth is shaped in producing sounds for certain letter cues (*sh, wh, th*, for example). The term *kinesthetic* refers to movement during sound production, the positions of the mouth, lips, and tongue. Teachers explain how sounds are produced and help children make distinctions between the sounds that they confuse. The point is to clarify sound production and relate it to the letters that represent those particular sounds. The instruction is explicit and often embedded in the child's point of confusion or need at the moment.

Mrs. Swanson is conferring with two boys who have completed a joint mural and each is writing a sentence strip about it. One boy indicates the next word he wants to write is *throw*.

MRS. SWANSON: *Throw, throw.* There are two letters that work together. Do you know what they are?

KESHAWN: *F*

MRS. SWANSON: They do sound like that. Listen, *frow* or *throw*?

KESHAWN: *O*

MRS. SWANSON: There is an *O*, but before that, there are two letters. Do you know the letters that start *THing* and *THistle*?

Silence.

MRS. SWANSON: (Writes *T* and *H*.) You are hearing *F.* (Writes *F.*) Say *fish.*

KESHAWN: *fish.*

Mrs. Swanson puts her teeth on her lip as if saying *F.* "Where are your teeth?"

KESHAWN: On my lip.

MRS. SWANSON: Say *throw.*

KESHAWN: *throw.*

Mrs. Swanson puts her teeth on her tongue as if saying *th.* "Where are your teeth?"

KESHAWN: On my tongue.

Mrs. Swanson points to her mouth. "Can you see the difference?"

In this strategy the child uses sight and touch in learning to hear and discriminate similar sounds. Possible teacher talk:

- Think about how that sound is made. Say the sound. How does your mouth move when you say that sound?

Strategy 7: Understand Variation in Complex Letter-Sound Relations

Many of the letter-sound relations in English are variable. This strategy stresses knowing the options and being flexible. The reader may have more than one option when working on a particular set of letters in reading. Vowel diphthongs, vowel digraphs, and the variable sounds of *C* and *G* are just some examples of more complex letter-sound relations. Teachers use brief directed lessons to develop these more complex concepts.

> DIPHTHONGS AND DIGRAPHS
> - Diphthong is a vowel phoneme that contains two sounds. Sound production glides from one part of the mouth to another (example: *boy*).
> - Digraph is a spelling of a sound (either vowel or consonant) with two letters representing a single sound (example: *flip*, *string*, *thing*). (Wilde, 1997)

Teachers' talk with readers after a lesson helps them recall the information and remember options. Strategy talk is about which choice to make. For example, in sounding out *giant*, a teacher might suggest when the hard sound is made as a first try, that the reader make the soft sound of *G*, the other option.

Teachers also help children see that some words are exceptions and do not correspond to general rules or expected patterns. The strategy for thinking about exceptions is seeing the departure from pattern. We observe a first-grade class studying a word pattern -*ake* (*take*, *make*, *rake*). As children suggest words, the teacher lists each one in a column with the -*ake* pattern printed in red. One child suggests that *ache* fits the pattern. When the word is written alongside the list rather than in the vertical column with the others, the teacher explains, "In this case the *C H* makes a *K* sound. It's one of those words that isn't spelled exactly the way you would think it is." Additional teacher talk options include:

- That letter can stand for more than one sound. Make it sound like ____ (mention words with the desired sound).
- This one is an exception. It is not spelled the way you expect.

Children's work with word sorts is a way to address these variable letter-sound relations. See Chapter Five for details of further word study instructional activities.

Strategy 8: Voice Print Matching to Focus Attention Word-by-Word During Reading

This strategy involves looking at the exact word that is being read and literally saying the word while focusing on it. Many first graders need support in this area. They need to focus on the correct word, understand the concept of one-to-one matching during reading, and realize the full potential of talk about letter-sound relations. Word matching may be complex for some beginning readers. There may be confusion about the concept of word and children may struggle to stay on the right word when words with multiple syllables are read. Voice print matching is often part of big book lessons, poetry reading, choral reading, and children's rereading of their own writing. Teacher talk may include:

- Point to each word as you read it. Keep your finger under the word you are reading.

Resources and Responsibility

An important support for children's independent reading and writing is the rich array of resources around the classroom. There are word lists, word walls, pattern charts, personal dictionaries, *ABC* word lists, neighbors that can help, and dictionaries, to mention just a few. Children are expected to use their resources—it's a matter of them thinking about what to do when they get stuck on a word and understanding that their task is to use the multiple resources around them.

In a sense, this resourcefulness is a strategy for independence. We observed teachers reminding children to use what they knew about language, letter-sound relations, and resources around the room as they worked. They reminded children of their options. JoAnne Lane reviews strategies before a writer's workshop.

MRS. LANE: What do we do after we start writing?

SAMMY: Look for a beginning, middle, and end?

MRS. LANE: What do you do if you're trying to make sense?

JANET: Ask your neighbor.

MRS. LANE: What do you do if you can't write a word?

CASEY: Sound it out.

MRS. LANE: You can stretch out the words. What else, do we have anything else in the room to help us?

FRANKIE: We have all kinds of words around the room to help us.

Strategies in Combination

So far in this chapter we have described strategies one at a time, providing examples and showing teacher talk. Our experience in watching teachers in action, however, has shown that talk about strategies often includes two or three strategies talked about or suggested in tandem. As teachers monitor children's reading, they point out the strategies that are being used. As children struggle, they suggest strategies to help.

To understand how strategies are talked about (used as a scaffold to prompt the reader or writer along) we notice the effort of both teacher and student. For example, in one of our observations, JoAnne Lane was supporting Tim's reading with a scaffold of questions that prompted useful strategies. They were reading in the middle of a book about the ocean.

TIM: (reading) Some are (self-corrects) some come in beautiful? (aside) No.

MRS. LANE: Does it make sense? Does it sound right?

TIM: Some come in beautiful bright colors. (He rereads to confirm, then continues reading fluently until he comes to the word *giant*.) Let me think of that word.

MRS. LANE: What do you do when you're stuck?

TIM: G G Is it long or short? [meaning hard or soft]

MRS. LANE: Try both. Which one makes more sense?

The reading continued in this conference. Tim did all the work and JoAnne prompted and supported his efforts by reminding him of strategies to use. She closed the session by confirming his actions, "I really like when you were rereading when it didn't make sense and you were using picture cues and sounds when you read." When we step back and think about this observation, we see that the teacher's scaffold supported the reader and guided his strategy use.

Ways to Teach Strategies

We have just shared teacher-student conferences in reading, writing, and guided reading lessons as instructional contexts for strategy instruction. Another powerful approach is the reading or writing demonstration. The teacher shares her thinking while writing a message or reading a story. She points to the print as she talks about the strategies she employs. She might show how she goes back to recheck a word and look closely at letters as she considers meaning. She might tell how she works on a word with a vowel digraph that is tricky and explain how she decides which letters to write. Often the demonstration includes children's participation as they suggest possible spellings for needed words. Here the level of engagement is high, the reading or writing is a meaningful text, and the demonstration contains explicit talk about strategies. (See Chapter Nine for a detailed description of writing demonstrations.)

Summary

The important understandings about strategies are:

- Strategies are partners for phonics skills and concepts.
- Strategies give children paths of action.
- The flexible use of skills and strategies is an essential part of children's reading and writing.
- Instruction needs to help children understand which skills and strategies to use when working with unknown words.

    The strategies described in this chapter are not a comprehensive list. They are meant as a sampling of common strategies that occur in instruction with beginning readers and writers. We review the list here with the hope that our readers will add to it.

- Use onset and meaning to figure out a word.
- Sound out a word by elongating its sounds in order left to right.
- Recheck writing by rereading and monitoring sounds.
- Use letter-sound information to rethink a miscue.
- Use pattern knowledge to figure out words.
- Monitor kinesthetic information.
- Understand variation in complex letter-sound relations.
- Use voice print matching to focus attention word-by-word during reading.

LINDA ORLICH:
TEACHER TO TEACHER

In my classroom, reading and writing are com-pletely intertwined. I believe that children learn to read through the writing program. I think of phonics as one wheel on the car to successful reading, and although it is a very important part, I teach other strategies as well. The embedding of the phonics instruction in a meaningful context, the connectivity of the skill focus, and the need to know on the part of the student allows the learner to develop the mental networks to use skills they've acquired in new reading situations.

Many times during the day I spontaneously slip in a minilesson as we read a story, as a child shares a project or writing, or as we record a science experiment. Tiny dialogues, multiple times during each day, connect the teaching moment to some skill I was trying to help the children learn. It happens across the entire curriculum. The little connectors are the glue that cement the formal lessons together—the bridges that help children reinforce what they already know and put new skills they are learning into a usable context.

My reading component is all literature. I have leveled books for instructional pur-poses, so the children can read successfully, but there is some challenge, too. In the morning, the children come in and choose a book from the leveled sets. They read it to themselves before school and during silent reading. As soon as they finish reading their chosen book, they go and pick something else for quiet reading. There are several hundred books from which the children can choose in the classroom.

When students read in class, they get support from their peers and from me to help decode or figure out unknown words. Usually they don't need much help. They may ask about one or two words. I would probably say ten percent of the children ask something every day. The rest of them don't ask anything. They just figure it out on their own. They've got all kinds of strategies to figure out unknown words.

Reading progress is tracked two ways. The first occurs when I listen to them read. I write down the level they're in and whether it's easy, challenging, or difficult. Sometimes I'll ask them a comprehension question or two about what they read. I try to vary the questions to get at higher level thinking skills, not just factual recall. I look for fluent reading. If the reader does not fly through the text with 95 percent accuracy or above, they don't really have a handle on it. Sometimes if they stumble through the story I'll wonder if they have any clue what they read. I'm amazed that sometimes they do know exactly what happened in the story. I don't know how they processed meaning when they stumbled that much through the book. I do running records once every nine weeks for sure. I do them more often with kids who are having trouble.

The second way I track reading progress is a reading journal where the children report the books they read at home. When the parents keep the log, I know Mom and Dad have a real good handle on the progress. There's no room for comments on the log, but there could be. I've often thought of providing room for parent comments on the take home log, but I want to make that reading homework as hassle-free as it can be. I know, as a parent, to find ten minutes to listen to your kid at night is sometimes a challenge, so I try to make it as painless as possible—just write down the title and the date, and that's enough. Sometimes parents will drop me notes and I'll write back.

We also keep writing portfolios. The rough drafts are more important to me than the finished products, so I save all the rough drafts. I save writing samples from every month or so. I'll just take a writing sample and stick it in there, so that I can see chronological progress. It comes in handy at parent conferences because we can look back at what their child did in the beginning of the year. It doesn't matter that everyone gets to point x; it's just how far you have come and if you are still moving.

Writing happens every day at some point. Some days we do class shared writing. The class helps compose a color rhyme for the day and records it on chart paper. Students later recopy the rhyme into their individual color rhyme books. Other days we have writers workshop where we're doing stories and we're writing. We do drafting, revising, editing. As the year goes on, that gets more intense. In the first half of the year, they're revising and editing with me. They may revise with peers, too, but not edit. In the second half of the year, when people get to be better spellers, they start editing with peers.

While the other children are doing independent work, the students who are ready to revise or edit come up to my desk one at a time. They read their drafts to me. I think that's where a lot of the reading instruction comes in, because you can really talk about it in the context of where they are so it makes sense to them. It's a lot harder for them to read what they've written two or three days later. The revision takes various forms. Sometimes the sentences don't hang together; there's stuff in there that doesn't make sense, and so, when they read it aloud, you say, "Oh, this doesn't make sense." Most of the time their writing does make sense. Usually they just need a little bit more at the end to bring it together, or to clarify something in a story. We do a lot of editing for spelling and sentence endings (usually periods).

I firmly believe that the children's needs and interests dictate when something is presented. The shared reading, the individual writing conference, the group story—all can provide opportunities for instruction, not an arbitrary sequence or planned performance. My job is to support and encourage their curiosity for knowledge, immerse them in print, and provide endless opportunities for exploration with books and writing.

5

Read, Write, and Learn About Letters, Sounds, and Words

JoAnne Lane's first graders are sitting on the carpet, reading a chart poem, and looking closely at the words chosen by the poet. They are wondering why *night* is not spelled *nite*. Aaron comments, "Maybe no one can answer this. Where does our language come from?" Amanda follows up with her own question, "Did God put words in our brain?" Although the questions appear humorous at first glance, they typify the inquisitive nature of children as they make sense of letters and words. Mrs. Lane celebrates such questions and responds without missing a beat, explaining that many English words actually come from other languages or are made up for new inventions such as computers. The discussion continues as the class thinks about words such as *byte*, *e-mail*, and *online*.

Teachers can celebrate and extend children's knowledge of letters, sounds, and words by building on their natural curiosity. In Mrs. Lane's classroom, children call themselves *word detectives*, and are eager to make new and important discoveries about the mysteries of the language they encounter in print. Their role as detectives casts them as active participants in learning experiences that extend, support, and answer their questions about words. For example, the students study charts of poems and songs looking for interesting spellings, compound words, contractions, rhyming words, and are always excited about new discoveries. In January, the children were amazed that *sleigh* and *reindeer* have a long *A* sound in the absence of an *A* in either word!

Some learning activities encourage children to observe, question features of print, and create their own agenda for word study. Other times, the teacher links words with the current classroom theme or closely examines groups of words the class may have struggled with while writing independently. Activities in which children are carefully examining and explaining word features are central to this chapter and have several unifying characteristics:

- The children are actively involved in manipulating letters, sounds, and words during classroom activities such as shared writing, shared reading, word gathering, and poetry study.

- Activities build on children's interest in words as they generate charts of related words, create new additions to their word study notebooks, or read thematic collections of books looking for words about a particular topic.

- The teacher selects word study activities based on observations and assessments of students' needs. The teacher's knowledge of each child guides decision making during individual conferences and while planning minilessons or other small and large group reading and writing lessons.

- Word study activities employ a variety of materials. These include chalk slates for writing word families, markers and large sheets of paper for creating class charts, word cards for sorting words using a pocket chart, or sentence strips to create sentences to cut-up and reassemble.

- Word study activities take place in a variety of settings. Whole group lessons may initiate writers workshop time. The teacher may call small groups together to study a particular feature such as long or short vowels. Word study also occurs during individual reading and writing conferences as the teacher provides instruction needed at that moment to help the child successfully read or write.

- Word study identifies the unique characteristics of English while looking for meaningful patterns and connections to support students' understanding of words.

This chapter focuses on how teachers can help children become more proficient readers and writers as they learn about the complexities of the English language. We look at:

- the contribution of the classroom environment to word study,

- and the instructional tools teachers select to meet the individual needs.

Word Study and the Classroom Environment

Children's inquiry about words may be inspired by their classroom surroundings as they create, add to, refer to, and study the words on display throughout the room. These displays not only create an exciting and attractive literate environment, they also provide a record of previous lessons and support children as they work independently.

Name Charts

At the beginning of each year, the teacher may create a chart of all the students' names in *ABC* order that serves as a reference point when talking about letters and sounds (Pinnell and Fountas, 1998). For example, in Mrs. Lane's room a name chart helps Sally connect her name with the *ABC*s displayed above the chalkboard and Sam, Sue, and Sally can discover that their names begin the same way. One name chart can hang near the writing center. A second one close to the large pad of chart paper is useful for shared or interactive writing. These name charts are easily accessible for children trying to decide which letter to use while writing a story. When the classroom theme is *Bears,* Bryan notices that *bear* begins like his name. Later in the year, the same name chart is a valuable resource to study more complex phonics concepts such as blends and digraphs (*Br* for *Brian; Ch* for *Chad; Sh* for *Shannon*). It can also help with endings such as the *Y* that sound like an *E* at the end of Kenny's name.

Word Families

Word families are a second way to organize and display word collections. A laundry line of paper shirts grows longer and longer in Mrs. Lane's room as the class adds a new garment for every word family they study (*can, fan, ran, man, pan,* and *tan; lunch, crunch, bunch, punch,* and *hunch;* or *make, fake, cake, rake,* and *take*). The display serves as a reference point for children as they read and write independently. The shirt collection creates a class word-pattern dictionary to supplement their personal dictionaries.

Other word charts can reflect the themes students are exploring. While preparing to write poems during a study of winter, Mrs. Lane's students brainstorm words that rhyme with *snow* and *fun* while the teacher writes the words on a large chart. As they create the chart, children discuss various spellings of rhyming words such as *fun, sun, done, ton,* and *none.* They mention *snow, whoa, hoe, toe,* and *slow.* The chart inspires children as they write their own poems about fun in the snow and also supports their spelling attempts.

Mrs. Lane's word collections also extend into math study as her children gather words that relate to numbers, shapes, and other math concepts. As they add to their collection throughout the year, they study connections between words with prefixes or roots based on mathematical concepts such as *tri-, bi-, poly-, deca-,* or *angle.* The meanings of these word parts not only support children as they learn math-related vocabulary, but also help them learn spellings of word parts as meaning units in a variety of words.

Sorting Letters and Words

Groups of letters or words in the classroom environment encourage learning through manipulation. Pocket charts or personal word and letter holders enable students to group and regroup letters, words, or even groups of words. Children can move magnetic letters on a cookie sheet or pizza pan to create many new words or place letters on the overhead projector so others can see their work. Groups of letters made of foam, plastic, or wood can be organized on cookie sheets or in tubs and other containers so children can create new and related words. Then, they record the words in their word study notebook or personal dictionary to keep as a resource and share with the teacher and other students.

Teachers can vary the level of difficulty for this work by adjusting the number of available consonants and vowels. One group of students may be challenged by a collection of letters consisting of one vowel and a group of consonants (*a, b, t, d, m, s, n*) and may create a variety of words like *sat, bad,* or *tan*. Other students may create more complex words with long vowel patterns when given the same letters with an additional *e* to make words such as *date, made,* or *bead*. Such open exploration of letters and words encourages creativity and offers many opportunities for learning about patterns and letter-sound relationships.

Word Wall

The class word wall is another learning tool for organizing the words children are learning to read and write. Word walls begin by writing each letter of the alphabet on a 3 × 5 note card. Teachers display the letters on a chalkboard or wall, leaving room below to add more cards with words the students are learning. The letter cards serve as headings to help children group words together that have the same first letter. Some teachers, with word walls made of magnetic surfaces, place small magnets on the back of each card so that children can move and manipulate the cards before returning them to the *ABC* order. When the word wall begins to fill, well known cards may be retired to a class word bank or placed in a class dictionary. Children use these resources to find words or word families and confirm their spellings while writing independently.

Student Dictionaries

Children's personal dictionaries are another way for them to collect and sort words they are studying. A dictionary can be as simple as a spiral notebook or sheets of paper stapled together. Inside, there are spaces to write special words in alphabetical order, to record groups of words from their word sort lessons, and to write groups of words from theme studies or word families. Each dictionary is personalized by the learner's entries and contains words selected by the child and words studied during lessons with the teacher. Lisa Dapoz purchases paperback personal dictionaries for each of her students. Each page has a list of ten or more words beginning with a different letter to help students write independently. The rest of each page has a generous space for children to write the words they have selected for each letter.

Dictionaries, word collections, word sorts, and environmental print focus children's attention on letters, sounds, and features of words and provide important support for children as they read new books and write new stories. Collecting winter words may assist students while reading a new big book about penguins. Generating sets of rhyming words may help them read a new poem. Personal dictionaries can foster independence during writers workshop and provide practice for words the child is not yet able to spell quickly or with ease. The links between word study, reading, and writing form an important support system to help children become increasingly independent.

Word Study Instructional Tools

In our teachers' classrooms, word study emerges not only from children's questions, interests, and comments but also during lessons specifically designed by the teacher to help children become increasingly more knowledgeable about how letters, sounds, and words work in reading and writing. Teachers conduct lessons in both small and large group formats and they use a variety of instructional tools, often in combination. In the sections that follow we describe a selection of lessons that are particularly helpful instructional activities as children learn to read and write.

I Spy with Poetry

Favorite poems are central to this word detective lesson as children search for special features found in words, lines, and verses. After Mrs. Lane's students reread their favorite chart poems for enjoyment and literary study, they revisit the poem as word detectives looking for relationships between words and studying the special words selected by the poet. The children often find rhyming words at the ends of stanzas and discuss the similarities and differences in their spellings. They also notice compound words, unique and unusual words created by the poet, or portions of the poems with alliteration or onomatopoeia. Cutting the poems apart by line or writing each line on a sentence strip enables students to *mix and fix* the poem, rereading to see if their version matches the original. Here are some sources for poetry study.

POETRY ANTHOLOGIES AND COLLECTIONS
Brown, C. 1998. *Polka-Bats and Octopus Slacks*. Boston: Houghton Mifflin.

Carlson, L.M. 1998. *Sol a Sol: Bilingual Poems*. New York: Henry Holt.

Cullinan, B. 1996. *A Jar of Tiny Stars*. Honesdale, PA: Boyds Mills.

Ebensen, B. 1986. *Words with Wrinkled Knees*. New York: Thomas Y. Crowell.

Hollyer, B. 1999. *Dreamtime: A Book of Lullabies*. New York: Viking.

Janeczko, P. 1998. *That Sweet Diamond*. New York: Simon & Schuster.

Nichol, B. 1997. *Biscuits in the Cupboard*. Toronto: Stoddart Kids.

Robb, L. 1995. *Snuffles and Snouts*. New York: Dial.

Sierra, J. 1998. *Antarctic Antics*. San Diego: Harcourt Brace.

Spinelli, E. 1999. *Tea Party Today: Poems to Sip and Savor*. Honesdale, PA: Boyds Mills.

Stevenson, R.L. 1998. *Where Go the Boats? Play-Poems of Robert Louis Stevenson*. San Diego: Harcourt Brace.

Word Play with Tongue Twisters

As students learn to appreciate the alliterative nature of stories and poems such as *Four Famished Foxes and Fosdyke* (Edwards, 1995) or *Faint Frogs Feeling Feverish* (Obligado, 1983), their interest grows in creating their own texts. The students in Lisa Dapoz's room create their own tongue twisters to share with their pen pals in another school.

- First, working in small groups, children select the initial sound and generate as many words as they can that begin with that sound.

- Next, each group shares their word collection with the rest of the class.

- Together students create a tongue twister by using the collection of words and the desires of the group.

During one writing session, the children drafted the following tongue twister: *Brandon, Brian, and Bryan discovered brown brachiosaurus and brontosaurus bones in Brazil.* Students then added phrases to use more words (*bridge* and *brains*) before finally settling on,

Brandon, Brian, and Bryan discovered brown brachiosaurus and brontosaurus bones and brains under a bridge in Brazil.

Other groups created similar tongue twisters, wrote them on large sheets of paper, drew illustrations, and put them together in a large book to send to their pen pals in their partner school. When the other class responded with their own tongue twister book, students used what they had learned to read the new messages.

BOOKS WITH ALLITERATIVE TEXTS

Edwards, P. 1997. *Dinorella: A Prehistoric Fairy Tale*. New York: Hyperion.

Edwards, P. 1996. *Some Smug Slug*. New York: HarperCollins.

Fleming, D. 1991. *In the Tall, Tall Grass*. New York: Henry Holt.

Enderle, J., and S. Tessler. 1997. *Six Sandy Sheep*. Honesdale, PA: Boyds Mills.

Jonas, A. 1997. *Watch William Walk*. New York: Greenwillow.

Most, B. 1998. *A Pair of Protoceratops*. San Diego: Harcourt Brace.

Most, B. 1998. *A Trio of Triceratops*. San Diego: Harcourt Brace.

Obligado, L. 1983. *Faint Frogs Feeling Feverish*. New York: Puffin.

Generating Lists of Words

Creating lists of related words provides substantial opportunities for word study and discussion of letter-sound relationships like the alliterative collections of words described previously. The collections may be student generated in school or at home. The children in Mrs. Lane's room have homework assignments to collect many different kinds of words. These assignments are exciting opportunities for families to talk about words and create lists that the children share the following day. For example, the children bring in lists of words that rhyme with *bear,* their current thematic study. They read many stories and poems about bears and are quite excited to bring in lists. The sharing begins as each child offers a new word and writes it on a word card while the class writes the word on their chalk slates. As the word cards are sorted into a class wall chart, they note both similarities and differences between words like *bear, care, fair*, and, of course, *Pierre*! The chart remains an important part of their room and helps children write their own rhyming poems. We share a word sort to demonstrate children's insights about relationships between words.

SORT OF WORDS RHYMING WITH BEAR

Hair	Delaware	pear	where	their	Pierre
lair	pare	wear	there		
pair	bare	underwear			
fair	fare	tear			
stair	scare				
air	mare				
chair	dare				
	stare				
	share				
	care				

Chalk Slate Lessons

Students in Mrs. Lane's room look forward to lessons using personal chalk slates (the size of 8 × 11 paper). Pieces of chalk are stored in an old sock, which then serves as an eraser. The slates are used for a variety of word play activities based on the word features students need to know. At the beginning of first grade, her students work on related letter shapes and then on simple rhyming words based on word families like -*at*, -*ill*, or -*ed*. Some days, the slates are divided into four squares with plenty of room to write a letter or word in each box. Later in the year, the students write words with more complex patterns:

- long vowel patterns *(-ide, -ain, -oat)*
- words with suffixes (adding -*ing* or -*ed* to known words and paying attention to doubling consonants)

Other lessons focus on making contractions or compound words, moving from one form to another so individual words like *will* and *not* become *won't* and the words *base* and *ball* become *baseball*.

The teacher selects the targeted word feature by studying children's writing and asking questions, "What are they using but are confusing?" or "What do they need to know to become more independent?" For example, Mrs. Lane noticed that students were not consistently using a *w* at the beginning of words like *was* and *went*, favoring instead a *Y*, the sound they hear at the beginning of that letter's name.

DECISION: Help children focus on words that begin with *Y* and talk about that sound.

The next chalk slate lesson focuses on words beginning with *Y* to help children learn that letter-sound relationship as they write words like *yak*, *yip*, *yam*, and *yarn*. Students suggest words that begin with *Y*.

Similarly, Janice Eddey plans a chalk slate lesson about short vowels when she notices that children are confusing the sounds of short *A* and *I*.

MRS. EDDEY: I'm noticing that the vowels are giving us trouble. We need to get our mouths ready to say these vowels. Practice saying *it* and think about the shape of your mouth. (She points to *it* written on the chalkboard).

Students say *it* slowly, emphasizing the first sound and write *it* on their individual chalkboards.

MRS. EDDEY: Now I want you to write *is*.

Students write *is* on their chalkboards.

The lesson continues as children compare and contrast the initial sounds of words including *is*, *it*, *at*, *and*, and *an* by listening to the teacher say the words, saying the words slowly, and writing each word on their chalkboard.

Word Sorting

During word sorting, students arrange and rearrange words in columns as they think about connections between groups of words. Sorts can be either teacher-directed or student-directed in large group, small group, or individual learning contexts. In a large group, for example, the teacher may assemble twenty words on the pocket chart in random order and invite students to work in pairs during their independent work time to organize the words in meaningful ways. Pocket charts are simply charts with several rows of folds in them. Each fold serves as a pocket that can hold cards for display. These charts are easy to make by folding chart paper horizontally in two or three places and stapling the folds.

Students can sort words for different purposes:

- word features (initial sounds, patterns, vowel sounds, number of letters)
- words connected by meaning
- words that are specific parts of speech (nouns, verbs, prepositions)
- any other way students can justify

Their sorts can be recorded in their word study notebooks and later shared in small or large groups. These sharing sessions support children's understandings about relationships between words and also provide a window for the teacher to understand the ways children are thinking about words, their spellings, use, and meanings.

Teachers organize more focused sorts based on the needs of a particular group of children. Closed sorts with children who are currently exploring the different sounds at the beginning of words may involve picture cards rather than word cards. The collection of pictures the teacher selects could begin with two distinct sounds, perhaps *B* and *S*. Children say the name of each picture and then decide if that picture should be sorted under the picture of the ball or the sun.

Other sorts may focus on words rather than beginning sounds. The teacher may work with a group of students to learn about long vowel patterns by creating a sort with words ending with silent *E* (*make, cane*) and those with two vowels together (*train, braid*). The word cards also include words with the same vowel sound but a different pattern (*weigh, day*) to add to the list of words not fitting the focus patterns. The cards with *make* and *train* served as the label for the two categories along with a question mark for words not fitting the pattern. Students discuss each word and note similarities and differences before placing it under the appropriate key word. Later, the cards can be reshuffled and resorted repeatedly moving toward doing the sort more quickly and accurately.

A more difficult sort occurs as the teacher or one student reads aloud the word on the card but does not show the card to the other students. Decisions are made about where to put the card without the benefit of spellings. Students can independently practice word sorting by mixing up the words and organizing them in pairs according to key words. Another approach is working in small groups and recording word sorts in a word study notebook or personal dictionary. Teachers can find examples of word sorts as well as extensive lists of words with particular features in several professional resources.

PROFESSIONAL RESOURCES FOR WORD SORTING

Bear, D. R., M. Invernizzi, S. Templeton, and F. Johnston. 2000. *Words Their Way: Word Study for Phonics, Vocabulary, and Spelling Instruction.* Upper Saddle River, NJ: Merrill.

Fountas, I. C., and G. S. Pinnell. 1999. *Voices on Word Matters: Learning About Phonics and Spelling in the Literacy Classroom.* Portsmouth, NH: Heinemann.

Ganske, K. 2000. *Word Journeys: Assessment-Guided Phonics, Spelling, and Vocabulary Instruction.* New York: Guilford Publications.

Pinnell, G. S., and I. C. Fountas. 1998. *Word Matters: Teaching Phonics and Spelling in the Reading/Writing Classroom.* Portsmouth, NH: Heinemann.

Sorting Words and Phrases

Pocket charts are helpful for sorting words and phrases into sentences to encourage children to create new meanings with different combinations. Phrases such as *I see the* can be linked with animal and color words to create real and fanciful sentences such as *I see the brown cow* or *I see the purple donkey* that children can use to write and illustrate their personal color book. Children can also sort mixed up words and phrases from familiar nursery rhymes or poems to reassemble the poem and check their work with the chart poem nearby.

During a thematic unit on animals, the children in Mrs. Lane's room make many new sentences by adding word cards with animal names to sentences on laminated strips.

A _____ is a small animal. But a _____ is the smallest animal of all.

Each new sentence is an opportunity to reread, checking to see if the words placed in the blanks make sense and reflect children's growing knowledge of animals and their characteristics. Such activities require children to look for familiar words, use beginning and ending sounds, and manipulate words and phrases to make meaningful texts.

Cut-up Sentences

An adaptation of the pocket chart word and phrase sorting previously described focuses on sentence strips created for groups of children to cut apart, mix-up, and reorganize. To use this lesson in a group setting, consider these options:

- Teacher and students generate and write a sentence on a chart or sentence strip. The teacher serves as scribe.

- Children may share the pen by providing the letters and words they know as they discuss how to write each word.

- Each child writes a sentence on a sentence strip.

- Teacher quickly types the sentence using the class computer and prints out copies for each child.

- Teacher may write the sentence and create the sentence strips ahead of time.

In the example following, Lisa Dapoz discusses the features of words in the sentence, *What did you do in school today?* by leading a game of "I Spy" before inviting the children to ask their own questions.

Mrs. Dapoz: I spy two words that rhyme. They sound pretty much the same.

Tom: *Do* and *you.*

Mrs. Dapoz: I spy vowels. See if you can find one with *I.*

Sally: *In.*

Mrs. Dapoz: I spy a word that can be spelled the same way forwards and backwards.

Andrea: *Did!*

Mrs. Dapoz: Right. I spy a word that rhymes with *cut.*

Jeanette: *What.*

> **Decision**: Focus children's attention on letter-sound patterns by having them look at the text and generate their own questions.

Mrs. Dapoz: Does anyone have another "I Spy"?

Bryan: What four words have the same vowel in them?

Jeff: *You, do, school,* and *today.*

Anne: What two words have *H* in them?

Joe: *What* and *school.*

After playing the game and rereading the sentence several times, it is cut apart. The parts are mixed up and students put the sentence back together again using what they know about words, letters, and sounds. Students write the sentence on an envelope and store their sentence inside for further work that night at home. The envelopes of cut-up sentences are inexpensive ways students can manipulate words and read with their family that night.

Studying Words Throughout the Day

The learning opportunities described in this chapter reflect the teacher's stance that word study is not confined to a brief time period each day, a set of worksheets, or a predetermined curriculum. Instead, children study letters, sounds, and words in reading and writing contexts throughout the day in ways that celebrate and support children's curiosity about words and how they work. The teachers in this book expect students to pose questions about letters, sounds, and words and follow up on such inquiries. But instruction is not limited to student questions. Teachers also base instructional decisions on their assessments of student work, create lessons to build on the knowledge students demonstrate, and extend that knowledge to increasingly more complex understandings. The teacher's in-depth knowledge of each child ensures that instructional time is not wasted on concepts children already know but, instead, focuses on moving children toward reading and writing increasingly more difficult texts.

A second important concept about word study instruction in these classrooms is the daily use of a variety of instructional settings. This includes students working independently or in pairs, teachers working with individuals, student-led small group work, and teacher-led small and large group work. This variety of instructional contexts provides multiple learning opportunities each day with specific attention to letters, sounds, and words. Attention to word study throughout the reading and writing experiences each day appropriately places word study within the context of children's daily reading and writing. This helps children deepen their understanding about phonics and spelling. These lessons embrace the challenge of teaching across multiple contexts and the complexity of following the child, resulting in a multi-thread tapestry of word knowledge.

JoAnne Lane:
Teacher to Teacher

Word study has always been an important part of
my teaching. I even did my master's thesis on
spelling. A big part of my motivation was based
on my belief that spelling, phonics, and reading
were obviously related and should be integrated.
But I struggled with the traditional weekly list of
spelling words and Friday tests. The kids knew the
words on Friday but not on Monday when they
wrote their stories. I wanted to show that you could
teach spelling based on kids' needs in meaningful
ways—there had to be a way! So, I read scholars
like Marie Clay, Sandra Wilde, Charles Read, and
Ed Henderson to develop a student-centered

spelling program. An essential part of my work focused on documenting my students'
knowledge of letter-sound relationships, which helped me plan for instruction.

I think that children learn by doing. So, all of the activities we do center on learning
to read by reading and learning to write by writing. Each day, the children have time to
read independently, read big books or chart poems with the rest of class, and read with
a friend. Then, I read with individuals and do running records so I can document their
progress and provide one-on-one instruction.

The same is true for writing. We write every single day. No matter what we're
doing, there's always some kind of writing involved. The children write with me in small
groups and also write their own stories. During independent writing, they help each other
by saying words slowly or finding the words they need in their personal dictionaries or
other resources in the room. Many times they work on their stories for several days in a
row before deciding to publish it and place it in our class library. The student-authored
books are definite favorites during silent reading!

Each day, we look for relationships between letters and sounds, among words,
across rhyming patterns, and also meanings between words. The children become just as
excited about words as I am and love to talk about their latest discoveries. The kids use
what they know about letters, sounds, and words in their writing.

I can remember being in school when subjects were kept in their place—you did
math and then that was put away; you did spelling and that was done for the day. Now,
we work to make things connect by working through themes and weaving reading and
writing into social studies and science. Our math journals are one cross-curricular example. We write in the math journals three or four times each week. When we are doing
patterns, for example, they create a pattern and describe it or they might write about
several ways to make five with colored unifix cubes. This way, they are learning math
and literacy at the same time.

Actually, there are many similarities between learning math and learning to read. We look for patterns in math and we look for patterns in words; we write words to communicate ideas and we write numbers to communicate ideas too—both must be clearly written and accurate! The word study in our classroom helps children see these patterns in so many ways: as we study rhyming words in our chart poems, as we work with word families with chalk slates, as we collect words with similar sounds, or as we study words through computer programs. Each part of our word study program is linked by the meaningful search for connections between what we know and what we want to learn about words.

We make many connections during shared reading of chart poems. Poetry has been a favorite genre of mine for years so I have lots of poetry books and many poems written on chart paper. The children love to read and reread the poems and make links with what they already know about words. We might talk about words that rhyme, compound words, contractions, words that begin alike, or words that sound alike but look different. Each discussion is shaped by the children's interests and my decisions to help them connect what they already know with new words. The poetry study continues as the children develop their own poetry notebook with their own copies of the chart poems we read together that they illustrate and keep in their notebooks. They love to read and reread their poems and often take the notebooks home to read to their family members.

Just as I studied about words for my thesis, my students learn about letters, sounds, and words by trying to find the answers to why words work the way they do. It's not always easy given the challenges of the English language, but it's so exciting to see six-year-olds make those critical connections as readers and writers when we explore our language together.

6 Shared Reading for Phonics Success

It is early morning in Alice Pleva's first-grade classroom. Children are seated on the carpet in the reading area, facing a chart stand displaying a poem. Mrs. Pleva is standing nearby with a pointer in her hand.

MRS. PLEVA: I notice a lot of you seem to like the poem about the snowmen, don't you? I see a lot of you writing about it.

CHILDREN: Read it again!

MRS. PLEVA: Read it again? Only if you'll help me.

Mrs. Pleva moves to the chart stand and begins reading. As she reads, she moves the pointer from left to right, pointing to individual words. Children join in the reading enthusiastically. At times, Mrs. Pleva hesitates and the children jump in with the rhyming word.

MRS. PLEVA: (reading aloud, pointing to the words)

Five little snowmen

On a winter's day

The first one said,

Wake up so we can (pauses)

CHILDREN: *play!*

At the end of the second reading, a child asks:

CONNIE: May I please have a copy?

MRS. PLEVA: You can make one. That's what some are doing. They're working in their journals on it, because our journals can be filled with poetry.

This scene represents one way a teacher supports her students' developing print and phonological awareness through shared reading of a predictable, rhyming poem, while also modeling what good readers do when they read.

One of the most effective ways to get young children involved with print is through the use of shared reading of enlarged texts. In shared reading, the teacher reads and the children actively participate in reading with the teacher's guidance. During this time the students and teacher gather informally in the reading area. Big books, chart poems, songs, and the children's own stories are read aloud, with the teacher pointing to the text as she reads. Children are encouraged to join in as they are ready, and they do so enthusiastically.

Shared reading with enlarged texts is the closest approximation to family storybook reading the teacher can offer for the whole group. It continues and builds on the literacy started at home. Inspired by the work of Don Holdaway (1979), activities with enlarged print help young learners to understand and experience what it means to be a reader. Children become aware of the concepts about print with teacher modeling (directionality, one-to-one correspondence, and spaces between words), and work on the sound structure of the English language (phonological awareness and phonics) through active participation.

In this chapter, we provide examples of various ways teachers use shared reading to support children's print awareness, developing phonological awareness, and growing phonics knowledge. These include shared reading with big books, chart poetry, songs, and the children's own stories.

Shared Reading with Big Books

To simulate storybook reading, many teachers use books with enlarged pictures and print. In choosing big books for shared reading, teachers need to consider several important factors. First, and most important, the book should be one that the children will want to read over and over again. Patterned and predictable language is a second key consideration for choosing a big book. The predictability of the language and plot make the story easy for young children to understand and remember. Patterns may be found in the rhyme or rhythm of the language, in the repetition of vocabulary or story structure, and in the storyline or shape of the story. Books with such patterns include:

- *Silly Sally* (Wood, 1992)
- *Polar Bear, Polar Bear, What Do You Hear?* (Martin, 1991)
- *I Know an Old Lady Who Swallowed a Fly* (Westcott, 1980)

Once students catch onto the patterns, they begin to recite the words and develop the confidence that goes along with this accomplishment. A third consideration is the size of the print. The text must be large enough so that each child will be able to follow the print as the teacher points to the words. Lastly, the teacher needs to consider the needs of the children and the purpose for reading as they select texts.

During shared reading, the book is read and reread many times. These multiple readings enable the child to explore more deeply the meaning of the story, as well as learn the visual and auditory language of the text. Different strategies may be used to strengthen and extend understandings. The teacher might talk about what the text means or discuss something the children noticed in the print or illustrations. Or, a book may simply be reread in unison, with children enjoying the pleasure of their own power of language and the accomplishment of knowing a book well. When most of the children are familiar with the story and begin to say the words and phrases of the book, the teacher focuses their attention on the print. Through explicit teacher talk, children learn print conventions and some sight words. When the students know some words, the teacher uses these words to begin to teach some letter-sound knowledge. As children learn to recognize more and more words in context, their ability to make analogies between familiar and unfamiliar words helps them figure out how to pronounce unfamiliar words by themselves (Moustafa, 1997).

Shared reading of a big book is a daily occurrence in Mrs. Pleva's first-grade classroom. Each morning the children gather on the carpet at the front of the room to listen and join in a shared reading of a favorite big book. Following the book introduction (title, author, etc.), children are encouraged to predict the story through the illustrations, then listen to confirm their predictions as the teacher reads. Mrs. Pleva often involves the children in cloze activities. These cloze activities encourage children to make meaningful predictions of words or phrases. Children make use of rhyme, repetition, and rhythm to fill in the anticipated language. In the example that follows, this procedure is demonstrated as Mrs. Pleva reads aloud from the big book version of *Who Sank the Boat?* (Allen, 1983). Because this book has both a repeating pattern, *Do you know who sank the boat?* and rhyme, it naturally invites children to join in the reading.

DECISION: Pause to encourage children to fill in the repeating pattern of text.

MRS. PLEVA: (reading aloud, pointing to the words)

Was it the donkey

who balanced her weight?

Who yelled,

'I'll get in at the bow before it's too . . . (pauses)

CHILDREN: *late.'*

MRS. PLEVA: (continues reading) *No, it wasn't the donkey*

who balanced her weight.

Do you ____ (pauses)

CHILDREN: (chiming in) *Do you know who sank the boat?*

Another instance of the cloze procedure occurs as Mrs. Abreu reads aloud from the big book, *The Snowy Day* (Keats, 1962). The teacher and children are at the point in the story where Peter, the main character, called in from playing in the snow, places a snowball in his pocket and goes inside the house.

DECISION: Encourage predicting of story events through questioning.

MRS. ABREU: What's he got in his pocket?

CHILDREN: A snowball.

MRS. ABREU: What kind of house is he going into?

CHILDREN: Warm.

MRS. ABREU: (reading continues) *He told his mother all about his adventures, while she took off his wet socks and he thought and thought and thought about them.*

MRS. ABREU: (later in the story) *Before he got into bed, he looked in his pocket. His pocket was* what? (pointing to the word *empty*).

CHILDREN: *Wet.*

DECISION: Validate a reasonable guess. Then demonstrate cross-checking meaning with graphophonic cues.

MRS. ABREU: It was wet! It sure was. There it is right there (pointing to the picture). *His pocket was* ____ (pauses) but this can't be wet, because it doesn't start with *w* (pauses, gets her mouth ready)

CHILDREN: *Empty*

MRS. ABREU: *His pocket was empty. The snowball wasn't there.*

Throughout the reading, Mrs. Abreu assists the children in monitoring for meaning through questioning and predicting and she helps them to use their knowledge of letter-sound relationships through crosschecking of visual cues.

Following a shared reading, teachers and children often revisit the text to search for particular sound patterns in words. For example, when Mrs. Abreu and the children finished reading aloud the big book, *When It Snows* (Nelson, 1992), they search for words that have a long O sound.

DECISION: Reinforce the silent *e* rule.

MRS. ABREU: I need you to focus in on the word *nose.* See if you can find the word *nose.* Spell it for me, Mark.

MARK: *N O S E.*

Mrs. Abreu writes *nose* on the whiteboard.

MRS. ABREU: Do you see an *O* in nose?

MARK: Yes.

MRS. ABREU: What sound is *O* making in *nose*?

MARK: *o* (making the long *o* sound).

MRS. ABREU: Long *O* because the *E* at the end makes the *O* say its name. The *E* is silent.

As additional words are found, they are recorded on O-Man, the Snowman, a snowman-shaped chart that is displayed in the room for ready reference. As the word search continues, the teacher and students talk about various patterns in words that make the long *O* sound, such as *ow* in *snow* and *oa* in *toast*.

Shared Reading of Poetry and Songs

Poems and songs in enlarged print on chart paper are shared with students in much the same way as big book stories. They provide young children with rich opportunities to hear the rhythm of language and develop phonological awareness of sound patterns. Certain poems and songs such as *On the Ning, Nang, Nong* in *Noisy Poems* (Bennett, 1987) invite readers to play with language. Through the use of nonsensical rhyme, rhythm, and alliteration, these poems invite language play and support developing phonological awareness. They also enable children of all backgrounds and cultures to actively participate as readers in a pleasurable, nonthreatening way.

Shared Reading of Children's Own Stories

When teachers and children write together in large group, they read (and reread) what is written. This familiar writing provides a purposeful and supportive context for shared reading. It also provides a meaningful context for explicit talk about how our language works, such as concepts of print, vocabulary, and spelling. Throughout shared writing, teachers and children stop often to reread what is written. They use all the cueing systems to check if their writing makes sense, sounds like English, and look at the spelling.

Skills and Strategies

Shared reading is a time when the teacher demonstrates reading and writing skills and strategies in meaningful, interesting contexts with active student participation. The teacher can use the supportive contexts of shared reading for a variety of purposes.

- Model and teach early concepts about print, such as directionality and one-to-one matching.

- Locate known words and letters.

- Predict letter-sound correspondence.

- Teach reading strategies such as rereading to think about meaning, anticipate what the meaning of the next section might be, and look at those new meanings in light of the story and its language.

- Teach about the information at the beginning of a book such as title, table of contents, author, and illustrator.

Skilled readers integrate the language cueing systems—background knowledge (semantics), structure of the language (syntax, grammar), letter-sound relationships (graphophonics)—to construct meaning from print. The teacher's goal during shared reading is to guide children successfully through this process. Understanding and applying the graphophonic cueing system is an essential component of the reading process. In school, most children acquire these necessary skills and strategies for successful reading and writing through demonstrations and participation with print during shared reading and through daily practice during writing time.

In addition to multiple rereadings, the teacher can use quick, focused activities to direct the children's attention to specific features of the text and to show them how to apply problem-solving strategies. Two possible activities are framing elements in the text and using a cloze procedure.

Framing Activities

Frames and questions help children notice specific concepts about print (Fisher, 1991). Teachers use prompts to direct children's attention to a particular aspect of the text. Teachers or students isolate the feature with a framing card (with a *window* in the middle of it). In the examples that follow, Mrs. Moore is playing "I Spy" with her children and framing words.

MRS. MOORE: Instead of my saying *I spy*, you tell me what you see, but first let's read it (the Daily News) together.

(The teacher and children read the Daily News in unison with Mrs. Moore pointing.)

MRS. MOORE: All right. You tell me what you see, Jamie.

Jamie frames the *Y* at the end of *cloudy*, but does not know what sound it represents.

DECISION: Name the letter for Jamie and emphasize the long *E* sound at the end of *cloudy*.

MRS. MOORE: Jamie has pointed to *Y* used as a vowel. What sound does it have? *cl-ou-d-Y*. What do you hear?

JAMIE: *E*

Framing activities can be used to locate an endless number of features in print:

- children's names
- rhyming words
- words that begin the same
- words that end the same
- compound words
- patterns within words

Cloze Procedure

Sometimes teachers use a cloze procedure to help children predict a word based on meaning and to apply crosschecking strategies to confirm or reject their prediction. A simple way to do this is by placing sticky notes over selected words throughout the text. The teacher reads the story up to the point where a sticky note appears and asks the children to predict the word. The teacher accepts and records all of their guesses. Pointing to each guess, she asks the children what letter they expect to see at the beginning of the covered word. Next, she uncovers the first letter of the word and the children confirm or reject their guesses based on that initial letter. Then, the teacher says the word slowly. Throughout this process, the teacher guides the children to use predicting, confirming, and crosschecking. The following is a specific example using the big book, *The Baby Who Got All the Blame* (Nelson, 1992).

MRS. ABREU: Boys and girls, I've covered up some of the words. I'm going to do the reading because this is our first time through the book. When I come to a word that's covered up, raise your hand if you know it. So, Stephan, you're going to do what good readers do when they read. You're going to use the ____ (pauses).

STEPHAN: Pictures.

MRS. ABREU: What else are you going to do?

MARK: Use the words that go in front of the word.

MRS. ABREU: So you're going to use all of the words in front of the word that is covered up. Patrick?

PATRICK: What makes sense.

MRS. ABREU: You're going to figure out what makes sense. What else are you going to do?

Susan: Use the rest of the sentence.

Mrs. Abreu: Use the rest of the sentence. Do I ever do that?

Children: Yes.

Mrs. Abreu: (begins reading the title) *The Baby Who Got All the Blame*
Make sure you can see the words.

This is Jake (reading aloud, pointing to the words).

Who made a mistake

When he opened the c (she has placed a sticky note over the word
except for the first letter). Adrian?

Adrian: *Cage* (looking at the picture).

Mrs. Abreu: *Cage.* What will be underneath here, if this word is *cage*?

Adrian: *A* and *G*.

Mrs. Abreu: So, we should have an *A* and a *G*. And (peeling back the
note) there it is.

Benefits of Shared Reading

Children enjoy shared reading because it enables them to be closely engaged with print. It offers a variety of benefits:

- enables children to gain confidence in their ability to develop as language learners and users
- provides needed support for less able readers who enter school with limited exposures to books and print
- offers a nonthreatening and enjoyable way to strengthen the language skills of struggling readers
- allows children to learn and participate at their own developmental levels and with their individual styles
- includes important experiences with children's literature

ALICE PLEVA:
TEACHER TO TEACHER

I love books! I figure if I love something, that carries over to my children. So, my first goal is to get them excited about learning to read and wanting to read. I read aloud throughout the day. There are so many wonderful books to choose from today; not like it was when I first began teaching twenty-some years ago.

I teach in a Catholic school and I'm required to use the basal series. However, it's my choice as to how these materials are used in my reading program. Our series is literature-based and there are many good stories to choose from, and having multiple copies is a convenience. Along with the basal [system of reading materials organized for instruction] I use a series of leveled texts [book sets organized by reading difficulty] and lots and lots of children's books for read aloud and choice reading. This is the children's opportunity to read from a variety of texts with adult supervision. Throughout the day, children may choose to read when their assigned work is finished. And, many days a week, we have DEAR time (Drop Everything And Read) where everything stops and we read. During this time, children may choose to read whatever they want. I read, too.

My read alouds are an important part of the reading program. I believe children grow in their love of books through the teacher's modeling. And I'm not the only reader. As the year progresses, we have many guest readers visit our classroom. One elderly woman from the parish visits weekly to read aloud to the children. The children also love it when Father Bill reads to them!

I've found children's literature to be a wonderful support for my phonics program. This year many of the children came to school not knowing the names of the letters of the alphabet and their sounds. A book can provide the context for teaching these skills. For example, I use Dr. Seuss books to help children become aware of rhyming patterns in words. We talk about word families and all the connections we can make knowing these patterns.

We write from the first day of school. We do a beginning-of-school dictated story together. We do this together, so they all go home the first day with a book. The children also have morning notebooks where they write and draw on topics of their choosing. However, I direct their writing journal topics. Often the writing is in response to a reading we have done. Or, it might be related to a topic we're studying in other curriculum areas. For example, when we studied Native Americans, I asked the children to write one new fact they learned about Native Americans. Sometimes we write together (brainstorming, listing, etc.). This provides another opportunity to talk about how words work.

Whenever possible, I try to go with the children's interests. Each week I choose a student of the week. That child brings his or her favorite book to school to share. Often their choice for sharing leads to an author study. This was the case when a book by Jan Brett was shared. We all became fascinated with the little hedgehog and this led to readings of many more Jan Brett books. It also supported our writing program because the children wrote letters to Brett asking questions about her books. Again, I had an opportunity to teach skills (letter writing) within the context of a meaningful, purposeful activity.

I like shared reading to be a relaxed time where children feel safe to jump in and try. The first reading is for enjoyment. I don't point to the words. We just read the story and get the meaning. During the second reading, I use my pointer and pause occasionally to see if the children can anticipate the needed word or phrase. Shared reading is a favorite time for the children and me. I think of it as our snuggle time. It truly is like the bedtime story with the children all up around me. I want this experience to be pleasurable and nonthreatening, a time when they view themselves as readers.

7

Lovely Literature
for Language
Learning

It is springtime and the children are in the midst of their study of bugs, birds, flowers, and other living things. Lisa Dapoz has a new collection of books to share with her first graders as well as some very exciting news—an author will be visiting their school soon, the very author who wrote these books! So begins the author study of Jerry Pallotta and his series of *ABC* books including *The Icky Bug Alphabet Book* (1986), *The Furry Alphabet Book* (1991), *The Flower Alphabet Book* (1989), and *The Bird Alphabet Book* (1989). As Mrs. Dapoz reads Pallotta's books, the class begins to notice and discuss some very important features of his work— all of the books use an *ABC* format; there's one letter of the alphabet on each page; and there's a different animal or critter on each page. During each read aloud experience, Mrs. Dapoz invites the children to listen actively to the text and predict the name of the animal, flower, or bug on each page, based on the letter of the alphabet and the picture. The *A* is for *ant*, the *B* is for *bumblebee*, the *C* is for *cricket*, and the *D* is for *dragonfly* but what is that mysterious bug on the *E* page? Why, it's an *earwig*. No one seems to know how it got its name!

Literacy scholars widely recognize the contribution of reading children's literature. Listening to stories and poems helps develop phonemic awareness and learning about letter-sound relationships. For many teachers, children's literature is central and essential to literacy instruction. They believe that reading children's literature and listening to stories and poems not only fosters enjoyment of literature, but also develops knowledge of letter-sound relationships. Their classrooms are filled with quality literature integral to daily teaching and learning activities involving books such as author studies, read alouds, big book readings, poetry circles, buddy reading, writers workshop, sustained silent reading, and thematic study. Phonics instruction is a consistent and significant pattern within literature study as children look closely at the ways authors and poets select words to tell their stories, write their poems, and experiment with language.

Examining the Writer's Craft

By focusing on the writer's craft, teachers can provide quality literature experiences and also encourage students to closely examine the characteristics of words authors use. The point is to foster appreciation for the text and enhance students' understanding of phonics concepts. Lee Galda argues for attention to the texts of stories fearing that "in our zeal to give readers and contexts their long-overlooked due, those of us concerned with children's developing literacy have recently ignored texts, acting as if they were incidental rather than as if they were just as vital to the construction of story as are readers and contexts" (1990, p. 248). She specifically encourages attention to powerful words author use and "delicious words and elegant sentences" found in quality children's literature. "Teachers and parents have the joyous task, the tremendous responsibility to provide children with the most interesting words, engaging sentences and intriguing text structures that they can find" (p. 255). Through studying the unique characteristics of texts in quality children's books, teachers give important instruction while supporting children's understandings about letters, sounds, and words.

The notion of a continuum may be a useful way to think of the contribution of children's literature to phonics learning. The special qualities of some books place phonics concepts at the center as children and teachers consider the author's craft. The alliterative qualities, for example, of *Some Smug Slug* (1996) by Pamela Duncan Edwards or *Watch William Walk* (1997) by Ann Jonas naturally inspire discussion of repeated sounds and letters authors use to create special moods and meanings. Listening to poetry encourages children to appreciate and discuss each poem's succinct language, rhythmic qualities, rhyming pattern, or other literary devises. Other books on the continuum may provide patterns to support students as they make their own books during writing workshop. While creating their own *ABC* books, for example, students will find helpful ideas about format and words in other alphabet books like Beau Gardner's *Have You Ever Seen . . . ?* (1986) or Reeve Lindburgh's *The Awful Aardvarks Go to School* (1997). Other books may provide an important backdrop for phonics teaching and learning. For example, reading or listening to multiple variations of folktales about the "Gingerbread Man" or the "Three Little Pigs" may inspire students' efforts to work with phonics concepts as they write their own stories.

ABC BOOKS
Arnosky, J. 1999. *Mouse Letters: A Very First Alphabet Book*. New York: Clarion.

Cahoon, H. 1999. *Word Play ABC*. New York: Walker and Company.

Chandra, D. 1999. *A is for Amos*. New York: Farrar Straus Giroux.

Cohen, I. 1997. *ABC Discovery! An Alphabet Book of Picture Puzzles*. New York: Dial Books.

Crews, D. 1967. *We Read: A to Z*. New York: Greenwillow Books.

Edwards, P.D. 1999. *The Wacky Wedding: A Book of Alphabet Antics*. New York: Hyperion.

Gerstein, M. 1999. *The Absolutely Awful Alphabet*. San Diego: Harcourt Brace.

Horenstein, H. 1999. *A is for . . . ? A Photographer's Alphabet of Animals*. San Diego: Harcourt Brace.

Isadora, R. 1999. *ABC Pop!* New York: Penguin Putnam Books.

Lester, A. 1998. *Alice and Aldo*. Boston: Houghton Mifflin.

Schwartz, D.M. 1998. *G Is for Googol*. Berkeley, CA: Tricycle.

Tobias, T. 1998. *A World of Words: An ABC of Quotations*. New York: Lothrup, Lee and Shepard.

Walton, R.1998. *So Many Bunnies: A Bedtime ABC and Counting Book*. New York: Lothrop, Lee and Shepard.

Wilbur, R. 1998. *The Disappearing Alphabet*. San Diego: Harcourt Brace.

The instructional ideas in this chapter are positioned at various points on the continuum described previously and provide insight into phonics instruction in the classrooms that we observed. The potential for learning about phonics through children's literature is described through key instructional opportunities that build on literary experiences to support students' achievement as readers and writers.

Children Learn About Phonics During Read Aloud Sessions

Read aloud time is typically a favorite part of the day, dearly loved by both teachers and students. The sheer enjoyment of sharing a favorite story or poem motivates both the reader and the listeners to a high level of engagement and involvement. Teachers sometimes select books with predictable patterns or refrains that invite students to join in during the reading. Other books appeal to students due to their humor, strong plot, interesting characters, or exciting climax. Some books may fit the class' current theme; others are favorites requested by the children or selected by the teacher to encourage children to be both enthusiastic and appreciative of quality children's literature.

The nature of some stories directs students' attention to sounds and letters while exploring the unique features of the text. Teachers may select these books to help children develop phonemic awareness, knowledge of letter names, an understanding of word patterns, or an inquisitive stance toward the relationship between sounds and letters. The poetic text of Phyllis Root's *One Duck Stuck* (1998) offers rich opportunities for children to hear playful, rhyming words as the forest animals arrive in groups to help the stuck duck. "Two fish, tails going swish, swim to the duck. Splish. Splash. No luck. The duck stays stuck deep in the muck down by the squishy, fishy marsh." Repeated readings of Root's text may support children's awareness of onsets and rimes, a foundational skill often linked with phonics understanding. Such stories help children listen for initial sounds and patterns. They are daily occurrences in Mrs. Dapoz's first-grade classroom as the students gather in the library corner several times each day to hear Mrs. Dapoz read a new story or reread an old favorite.

The class explores letter names and sounds when Mrs. Dapoz shares a holiday favorite, *The Christmas Alphabet Book* (1994) by Robert Sabuda. Each page of the pop-up alphabet book has two doors which, when opened, contain a pop-up of a Christmas symbol beginning with a letter of the alphabet. The children enthusiastically predict several holiday words such as Santa, star, and snowflake for each letter of the alphabet before celebrating Sabuda's choice and appreciating his talent for creating intricate cut paper pop-ups.

Read aloud time is also a learning experience about letters, sounds, and rhymes when Mrs. Dapoz shares *Miss Bintergarten Gets Ready for Kindergarten* (Slate, 1997). To begin, she asks the children what they notice about the title and the endpapers. They quickly note the rhyme in the title and colorful *ABC*s on the endpapers. As Mrs. Dapoz reads, the children notice the *ABC* order at the beginning of each sentence describing one child in Mrs. Bindergarten's class and identify the pattern of rhyming words in the text. By hesitating at the end of reading, "Brenda Heath brushes her ____," Mrs. Dapoz invites the children to guess, "teeth!" They continue predicting rhyming words throughout the 26 members of Mrs. Bindergarten's class. Through stories like this, children learn about letter names, the *ABC* order of the children's names, how the names related to children in their class, and the rhyming patterns on each page.

Author studies are also opportunities for studying the special characteristics of a single author by looking across a variety of titles. Many of Bruce McMillan's photoessays and concept books, for example, have accompanying text that plays with language in enjoyable and unique ways. McMillan's alphabet book, *The Alphabet Symphony: An ABC Book* (1989), explores the shapes of letters through the lens of his camera aimed at an orchestra. In *Puniddles* (1982), McMillan matches pairs of photographs which, when combined, offer new meanings to the words represented by individual pictures. McMillan's use of pairs continues as he explores two-word sentences in *Puffins Climb, Penguins Rhyme* (1995) and additional pairs of rhyming words in his terse verse books, *One Sun* (1992) and *Play Day* (1991).

When Mrs. Dapoz's class studies McMillan's work, she introduces *One Sun: A Book of Terse Verse* saying, "I'm going to show you the picture and you have to guess the rhyme. It's going to be a two-word rhyme." Each two-page spread features McMillan's color photograph illustrating a terse verse written on the opposite page. Mrs. Dapoz provides several hints as the children identify the rhyme for the first photograph of sand covering a child's hand as a *sand hand*. The activity continues as the children identify the *lone stone, snail trail,* and *six sticks* by predicting the rhyme and confirming their guess through examining the words on the opposite page. Through such activities, children are actively involved in the books, generating multiple possibilities, and thinking hard about potential rhyming pairs of words.

AUTHORS WHO PLAY WITH WORDS

Edwards, P.D. 1995. *Four Famished Foxes and Fosdyke*. New York: HarperCollins.

Edwards, P.D. 1997. *Dinorella: A Prehistoric Fairy Tale*. New York: Hyperion.

Edwards, P.D. 1996. *Some Smug Slug*. New York: HarperCollins.

Edwards, P.D. 1999. *The Wacky Wedding: A Book of Alphabet Antics*. New York: Hyperion.

McMillan, B. 1995. *Puffins Climb, Penguins Rhyme*. San Diego: Gulliver.

McMillan, B. 1991. *Play Day: A Book of Terse Verse*. New York: Holiday House.

McMillan, B. 1990. *One Sun: A Book of Terse Verse*. New York: Holiday House.

McMillan, B. 1989. *The Alphabet Symphony: An ABC Book*. New York: Apple Island.

McMillan, B. 1982. *Puniddles*. Boston, MA: Houghton Mifflin.

Most, B. 1992. *Zoodles*. San Diego: Harcourt Brace.

Most, B. 1998. *A Pair of Protoceratops*. San Diego: Harcourt Brace.

Most, B. 1998. *A Trio of Triceratops*. San Diego: Harcourt Brace.

Most, B. (1999). *Z-Z-Zoink!* Orlando, FL: Harcourt Brace.

Slepain, J., and A. Seidler 1990. *The Hungry Thing Returns*. New York: Scholastic.

Slepain, J., and A. Seidler. 1967. *The Hungry Thing*. New York: Scholastic.

Ziefert, H. 1997. *Night Knight*. Boston: Houghton Mifflin.

Ziefert, H. 1997. *Baby Buggy, Buggy Baby*. Boston: Houghton Mifflin.

Homophones pose unique phonics challenges to young writers trying to understand how words can sound the same but are spelled differently with varying meanings. Books like *A Chocolate Mousse for Dinner* (1976) by Fred Gwynne, Guilio Maestro's *What's a Mite Might?* (1986), and Peggy Parish's *Amelia Bedelia* books offer enjoyable ways to learn about this difficult concept.

Mrs. Dapoz introduces Fred Gwynne's *The King Who Rained* (1988) by linking it to a conversation she and the class had about the words, *tow* and *toe*:

> I found a really funny book that I think you will like. Remember how we spelled *tow* and then somebody pointed to their *toe*. Those are called homophones. This is called *The King Who Rained*. Does anybody get this one? (refers to the picture and explains the difference between *reigned* and *rained*.)

Mrs. Dapoz and her students enjoy Gwynne's playful text about forks in the road, a mole on Daddy's nose, and painting the house with two coats. They pause to discuss the way the spelling of the words affects the meaning of the sentences. This invites children to be very attentive, looking closely at the pictures and volunteering to explain each picture after attending to the spellings of each pair of homophones.

BOOKS ABOUT HOMOPHONES, IDIOMS,
AND OTHER TRICKY KINDS OF WORDS

Gonennel, H. 1994. *Odds and Evens*. New York: Tambourine.

Gwynne, F. 1976. *A Chocolate Mousse for Dinner*. New York: Simon and Schuster.

Gwynne, F. 1988. *The King Who Rained*. New York: Simon and Schuster.

Maestro, G. 1984. *What's a Frank Frank?* New York: Clarion.

Maestro, G. 1986. *What's Mite Might?* New York: Clarion.

Parish, P. 1963. *Amelia Bedelia*. New York: Scholastic.

Parish, P. 1971. *Come Back, Amelia Bedelia*. New York: Harper and Row.

Parish, P. 1972. *Play Ball, Amelia Bedelia*. New York: Scholastic.

Parish, P. 1979. *Amelia Bedelia Helps Out*. New York: Avon.

Parish, P. 1981. *Amelia Bedelia and the Baby*. New York: Avon.

Terban, M. 1982. *Eight Ate*. New York: Clarion.

Terban, M. 1983. *In a Pickle*. New York: Clarion.

Terban, M. 1985. *Too Hot to Hoot*. New York: Clarion Books.

Terban, M. 1986. *Your Foot's on My Feet!* New York: Clarion.

Terban, M. 1987. *Mad As a Wet Hen!* New York: Clarion.

Terban, M. 1988. *The Dove Dove*. New York: Clarion.

Terban, M. 1988. *Guppies in Tuxedos*. New York: Houghton Mifflin.

Terban, M. 1990. *Punching the Clock*. New York: Clarion.

Ziefert, H. 1997. *Night Knight*. New York: Houghton Mifflin.

Ziefert, H. 1997. *Baby Buggy, Buggy Baby*. Boston: Houghton Mifflin.

Books like *Q Is for Duck* (Elting and Folsom, 1980) encourage a similar level of student involvement during read aloud time. The title exemplifies the book's pattern. Children enjoy explaining that *Q* is for *duck* because ducks quack and *B* is for *dog* because a dog barks. As the teacher reads this book aloud, children listen closely as each of the 26 patterns are opportunities to link beginning sounds to a meaningful connection with another word.

Nearly every day during read aloud time, children can listen to stories like those previously listed that focus their attention on the sounds of language and the relationships between letters and sounds. This attention to phonics concepts while the teacher is reading may enhance both students' appreciation of the author's craft and their knowledge of words, letters, and sounds. As they listen, children are actively engaged in the stories and often express their enjoyment of the books through their obvious attention to the stories and requests to read it again.

Children Learn About Phonics Through Poetry

Poetry holds a very special place in the classrooms in this book. Poems are shared from collections, written on chart paper, read chorally with varying voices for effect, and enjoyed in big book format. In Mrs. Dapoz's room, the children enjoy poetry circles, a time when each student prepares a favorite poem to read expressively to the others. Students often initiate this activity and respond with excitement when Mrs. Dapoz announces that they will have a poetry circle the next day. Children immediately go to the library corner with some sticky notes to mark and practice favorites for sharing. While reading and listening to poems, children enjoy the succinct, powerful words of the poets and the sounds poets employ for special effects.

JoAnne Lane writes many poems on chart paper in print large enough for everyone on the carpet to see. Other poems are displayed on colorful charts hanging on an easel. These texts are a central component of the class' daily shared readings. After the children read and reread the poems and enjoy the language of the text, they are encouraged to notice the features of words the poet used. In November, the students read and sing a Thanksgiving version of "I'm a Little Tea Pot" that their teacher had written on chart paper.

> I'm a little turkey
>
> look at me.
>
> Fat and plump as I can be.
>
> Don't you try to catch me
>
> Cause, you see
>
> I'll hide behind this
>
> old oak tree.

When invited to look closely at the words and talk about what they noticed, the children note several contractions and some rhyming words (*me, be, see,* and *tree*). Next, the children identify the long *E* sound in those rhyming words, connect the words with turkey in the first line, and discuss the variety of spellings they find. Their interest in this feature continues as they link the words with the spellings of children's names in their room—Katie and Sydney—and discuss ways they can use letters and sounds as they write poems during writer's workshop.

Poems may also inspire children to write variations of well-loved nursery rhymes. Based on their familiarity with "Hickory Dickory Dock," Mrs. Dapoz poses the question, "What if the clock struck two?" which begins the shared writing of their own version.

> Hickory, dickory dock.
>
> The mouse ran up the clock.
>
> The clock struck two.
>
> The mouse said, "O-o-o-h!"
>
> Hickory, dickory dock!

> Hickory, dickory, dock.
>
> The mouse ran up the clock.
>
> The clock struck three.
>
> He lost his key.
>
> Hickory, dickory, dock.

Mrs. Dapoz serves as scribe as the children generate each new line and the appropriate rhyming words. As they compose, the class carefully considers poetic devices required for their new poem by discussing the rhythmic pattern of the original verse and the poet's use of rhyming words. The spellings of individual words provide instructional opportunities for phonics concepts such as initial consonants, vowel patterns, digraphs, and blends.

As teachers share poetry with students in the ways described previously, multiple curricular goals may be accomplished. Poetry readings develop an appreciation for careful word selection and succinct meaning, creating an early love of poetry in young readers.

- Opportunities to read and reread poems in large print formats provide successful reading experiences for children as they enjoy the poet's craft and the choral reading.
- Reading and writing poems draws children's attention to the details of words and offers learning opportunities that support phonemic awareness and the development of phonics concepts.

POETS TO STUDY WHO PLAY WITH WORDS

Adoff, A. 1988. *Chocolate Dreams*. New York: Lothrop, Lee and Shepard.

Adoff, A. 1979. *Eats: Poems*. New York: Lothrop, Lee and Shepard.

Adoff, A. 1991. *In for Winter, Out for Spring*. San Diego: Harcourt Brace.

Adoff, A. 1995. *Street Music: City Poems*. New York: HarperCollins.

Florian, D. 1994. *Beast Feast*. San Diego: Harcourt Brace.

Florian, D. 1997. *In the Swim*. San Diego: Harcourt Brace.

Florian, D. 1998. *Insectopedia*. San Diego, CA: Harcourt Brace.

Florian, D. 1999. *Laugh-eteria*. San Diego, CA Harcourt Brace.

Lewis, J. P. 1998. *The Little Buggers*. New York: Dial.

Lewis, J.P. 1998. *Doodle Dandies: Poems That Take Shape*. New York: Simon and Schuster.

Lewis, J.P. 1999. *The Bookworm's Feast: A Potluck of Poems*. New York: Dial.

Theme Projects, Literature, and Phonics

Children's literature also serves as a central component for lengthy thematic studies in the first grades we feature here. Books are the "glue" connecting reading and writing with content areas such as science, math, or social studies. When the class studies color and light, Mrs. Dapoz selects *My Many Colored Days* (1996) by Dr. Seuss to read aloud. She introduces the book by connecting their science topic with an appreciation of Dr. Seuss's word choices and its potential contribution to students' independent writing:

MRS. DAPOZ: Since we are talking about color and light and how light is made up of many colors, I thought I would read this. What I like about this book is how Dr. Seuss thinks of color and thinks of his moods. Later in writers workshop you might want to make a color book that tells how you feel on a blue day or an orange day. I like Dr. Seuss's books because they always rhyme. You can help me out and kind of chime in when you come to a part where it rhymes and you can figure out what Dr. Seuss wrote.

Discussion throughout the reading focuses on Seuss's rhyming words and the relationship between color and mood as illustrated in both the text and pictures, thus providing cross-curricular learning opportunities. This lesson reinforces reading concepts such as rhyming words while enjoying a quality piece of literature, and studying color and light.

Collections of books also offer opportunities for children to make intertextual connections across books and curricular areas. Mrs. Dapoz's collections relate reading and writing activities that draw in phonics connections. While studying nursery rhymes at the beginning of the year, the children listened to poems, read enlarged copies during shared reading, and wrote original verses during shared writing. Later in the year, they enjoyed Mrs. Dapoz's collection of tongue twister books and generated their own to share with their pen pals at a different school.

COLLECTIONS OF NURSERY RHYMES

Agard, J., and G. Nichols. 1995. *No Hickory No Dickory No Dock.* Cambridge, MA: Candlewick Press.

dePaola, T. 1985. *Tomie de Paola's Mother Goose.* New York: Putnam.

Foster, J. (Comp.). 1996. *First Verses.* New York: Oxford University Press.

Lobel, A. (Ed.). 1986. *The Random House Book of Mother Goose.* New York: Knopf.

Opie, E., and P. Opie (Eds.). 1988. *Tail Feathers from Mother Goose: The Opie Rhyme Book.* Boston: Little, Brown.

Opie, I. (Ed.). 1996. *My Very First Mother Goose.* Cambridge, MA: Candlewick Press.

Opie, I. (Ed.). 1999. *Here Comes Mother Goose.* Cambridge, MA: Candlewick Press.

Prelutsky, J. (Ed.). 1988. *Read-Aloud Rhymes for the Very Young*. New York: Knopf.

Wildsmith, B. 1963. *Brian Wildsmith's Mother Goose*. New York: Watts.

An extended reading and writing connection with literature takes place in Mrs. Dapoz's classroom using her collection of stories about Jack and his beanstalk. Late one night, Mrs. Dapoz places a large flower stalk in a cup where the children had planted flower seeds. The next morning, the mysterious presence of this gigantic flower combined with the display of *Jack and the Beanstalk* variations and a brief letter signed "Jack" leads to an ongoing drama about Jack visiting their classroom at night trying to hide from the giant. Daily, the children read and listen to stories about Jack and respond to Jack's evening letters by writing their own class notes and individual messages. Initially, the children write letters to other classes explaining the amazing visitor's presence in their room and warning the others that the giant may soon follow. When one of Jack's evening messages reveals the giant is discovering his hiding place in the classroom, the children create a note to the giant in an attempt to distract the giant from his prey.

Dear Mr. Giant,

You don't smell Jack. You smell our lunch. We haven't seen Jack in eight weeks. The last time we saw him, he was heading for the sewer. We promise.

Sincerely,
The Detectives

The children also wrestle with the ethics of Jack's theft of the giant's possessions and create charts revealing their votes in favor of returning the goods to the rightful owner. Soon, the room and outside hallways are filled with charts, stories, and individual letters.

Each piece of writing presents opportunities for phonics instruction as the children work through the conventional spellings of words to communicate with Jack, the giant, Jack's mother, and the rest of the school. Motivation to read and write is high with a similar level of student involvement as they read messages left by Jack and the giant each morning and create their individual and collective responses.

Across the curriculum, carefully selected children's literature inspires such activities and accomplishes multiple learning goals simultaneously. The enjoyment of a quality book lends itself to a variety of reading and writing activities as children learn about content areas such as science and math or extend their abilities to write using their growing understanding of phonics concepts.

Conclusion

The continuum of instructional opportunities described in this chapter serve the dual purpose of celebrating the writer's craft and teaching more about letters, sounds, and words within the context of rich literature experiences. Our recommendations must not be interpreted as confining literature study to only those books supporting phonics learning. Instead, the learning opportunities in this chapter are intended to be embedded within a much larger, more comprehensive literature-based curriculum including wide reading of quality books from a variety of genres every day. Certain books, however, create teachable moments during which phonics instruction can become one facet of the talk about the book.

The key to quality phonics instruction with children's literature is an enthusiastic teacher with a strong knowledge of children's books, an appreciation for authors' careful word selection, and the ability to invite children into the world of "delicious words and elegant sentences" (Galda, 1990).

LISA DAPOZ:
TEACHER TO TEACHER

For the past nineteen years, I've worked with first graders to support children's inquisitive nature about how language works and to study language features to help them read and write. Every day we celebrate learning something new as we read and write together. My philosophy is to present meaningful experiences for children using whole texts and emphasize the very best children's literature. Great books are in every nook and cranny of my room! One large display houses informational books related to our current theme. The front of each book is displayed inviting children to visit and revisit each one. Other collections of books are found in plastic crates labeled so children can easily find just the right book. I have sets of folktales, poetry, *ABC* books, number books, and also books grouped by author or illustrator, which children can explore as they look for more and more books to read. Our in-class library collection includes books children can read independently as well as more difficult picture books or chapter books they can read with their third-grade buddy readers, take home to read with the family, or read independently.

I always try to make lessons meaningful and complete experiences by using whole pieces of text. My children are immersed in opportunities to read and write for hours each day through read aloud sessions, shared reading and writing, interactive writing, computer writing, independent reading, writing workshop, and the children's daily book-in-a-bag shared each night at home. I find that certain reading times become favorites—like the day one young boy expressed his concern that we had not had a poetry circle lately. When I responded that we would have one the next day, he became very excited and quickly moved into the classroom library saying, "Got to go get some poetry!" He scoured his favorite poetry books before selecting just the right poem to prepare for sharing the next day with his classmates.

Our library corner is an important part of literacy instruction each day as children gather to listen and discuss. Some of the books I pick are great opportunities to talk about rhyming words, word families, letters and sounds, or *ABCs*. Lots of phonics instruction goes on during read aloud time. However, the library corner is also an important setting for my students' independent reading. There, they find tubs of books organized according to reading levels, genre, and theme to help them locate just the right book for SSR (sustained silent reading) time or to take home that night to read to family members. Often, they pair up with a friend to enjoy reading their books in a cozy spot on the carpet.

In our library corner, we also read chart poems and big books and write together on large sheets of chart paper. One day, for example, we created a thank-you note for a recent guest speaker. First, we talked a lot about what the children wanted to write. Then, we shifted to spelling each word as I wrote on the paper. I knew which words they could write independently so we didn't spend much time on those. Other words, however, were important times for in-depth discussions about word features like initial and final consonants or vowel patterns. I see these lessons directly transfer into their independent writing so that what they do with me on one day might be done on their own the next.

I think of phonics like a spider web; it may look fragile, but there's a real system and organization to it. It's supportive; it's cyclical; it's reinforcing. We keep going back to things we know to learn something new. I usually know when kids are ready for my help figuring out something like a silent *E* or adding -*ing*. My years of experience help me know what teaching will build on what they already know but move their knowledge ahead. Teaching phonics while kids are listening to stories, reading independently, and writing their own stories helps them make those spider-web connections and to use what they know about letters and sounds while they read and write.

Writing Workshop for Tailor-Made Phonics Instruction

8

When children write, they think about and often extend their phonics knowledge. Writing opens the gate for attempts at new words and helps children apply phonics concepts from recent classroom reading and writing activities. Previous reading experiences focusing on letter-sound patterns, word study lessons, and personal knowledge of encoding patterns all have the possibility of coming into play.

Writing time also provides occasions for tailor-made phonics instruction. When children select a particular word and make an effort to represent its sounds, engagement is high. Teacher-student interactions focusing on the needed letter-sound relations for such words provide experiences for phonics growth. They are a significant strand of the phonics instruction that children can receive during writing experiences. In fact, when this kind of instruction surfaced as a major pattern in our phonics research, we called it *phonics at the point of use*. The key idea is that such impromptu phonics instruction helps children progress developmentally in phonics knowledge. Rather than being mere scraps of phonics information with little instructional value, these one-on-one interactions during writing experiences help build phonics concepts and strategies that are used immediately.

In this chapter, we look at writing workshop as a time in which phonics instruction plays a significant role. In writing workshop, phonics knowledge is called upon and instructional opportunities that address specific phonics concepts and strategies occur. The challenge in this instruction is to keep the art of writing as the central focus and present phonics concepts as essential, supportive information. To see how this is done, how informed teachers juggle these two areas simultaneously, we focus on the decisions teachers make as they work with children's writing.

We note one caveat before we begin. The instruction we describe takes into account the nature of the drafting process in relation to phonics knowledge. Children often do not show what they know about letter-sound relations when they are in the midst of writing. Their attention is divided as they simultaneously grapple with what to write and how to get that meaning written. Known words and patterns are sometimes missed and phonics concepts from recent instruction may or may not show up in the initial drafting process. The gap between what children know about written language and what they actually produce in drafting is often significant. Certainly, this gap is part of the reality of children's work in the writing classroom. As teachers, our task is to work with this reality. We can help children take a second look at their writing and recall the letter-sound patterns they know. Another part of our task is to provide instruction in new phonics concepts and strategies that children need as they write.

Writing Workshop and the Teaching of Phonics

Several kinds of encoding support can be provided without disturbing the primary emphasis in writing workshop programs. We expect that minilessons will address aspects of the writer's craft such as how to write leads and how to focus on a particular topic or point. In addition, there may be occasional minilessons in children's writing, conferences that address letter-sound patterns needed in current drafts, and supportive materials around the room that provide letter-sound information for writers at work.

Minilessons in Writing Workshop

Minilessons can address children's common encoding difficulties and present information about needed letter-sound patterns. A spot check of various spelling miscues across a day's writing provides an excellent basis for brief lessons focused on encoding issues. These minilessons may involve individual chalkboard work where children write dictated words, discuss what they notice, and how particular words were figured out. The minilessons may feature the teacher demonstrating particular spelling strategies or letter-sound patterns.

MINILESSONS

- Discuss short vowel patterns as children write dictated words. Children use individual chalkboards and the teacher dictates words by pattern.

- Arrange words in lists according to vowel sound to discuss contrasts between one short vowel pattern and another. The teacher leads a discussion of each word.

- Study the silent *E* pattern by adding an *E* to dictated words and talking about the medial vowel sound. Children write *at* then add an *E* and say the new word *ate*; they change *pin* to *pine*, *rod* to *rode*.

- Sort short and long patterns of the same vowel and write them in lists. Children nominate words for each list and discuss whether nominations fit the short or long vowel pattern.
- Dictate words to fit specific patterns (-*ame*, -*ake*). Children write dictated words on individual chalkboards.
- Add -*ed* endings to words that children nominate. The teacher demonstrates how to add these endings.

Minilessons provide a useful focus for phonics follow-up work with individual writers. In editing conferences where conventional spellings are addressed, the same encoding patterns talked about earlier in mini-lessons are pointed out again. Our classroom observations show that even fairly advanced writers seem to miss the connection between concepts talked about instructionally and the editing they personally need to do. The teacher builds this connection by reminding students of the minilesson and then helping them find instances of that pattern in current work.

Conferences That Address Phonics Concepts

In many workshop programs, conferencing serves as one of the key sources of writing instruction. Teachers work with the issues that are most pressing and try to help as many writers as possible in a given period. Janice Eddey reflects on the role of phonics in her writing conferences.

> I think children learn phonics when they're writing. In reading they can use different strategies, like what makes sense, how I would say it, and looking at the picture. All those support letter-sound work in decoding when children are reading. But when children are encoding in their writing, the only real thing they have is what they know about letter-sound relationships and what they intend to say. When I assess the children, the number of sounds they hear in words correlates with their progress in reading as well as writing.

Mrs. Eddey offers three kinds of conferences for young writers. Each type of conference potentially includes attention to the writer's encoding problems as well as other writing issues.

- *Help Conference*—The teacher circulates among writers at work and provides help encoding.
- *Revision Conference*—The teacher works with writers on revision and talks about letter-sound relations in their writing.
- *Editing Conference*—Teacher and student look at a completed draft for spelling and punctuation.

To elaborate on how these conferences are conducted and focus on the teacher's role, some classroom examples are provided in the following.

Help Conferences   Mrs. Eddey is working with Michael who is writing a first draft and needs to spell *jungle*. He has written *gagol*.

> **DECISION**: Emphasize the vowel sounds to see if Michael can connect an earlier lesson that day with his own work.

MRS. EDDEY: Let's try jungle again. What vowel says *u*?

MICHAEL: *U? A?*

MRS. EDDEY: Like *umbrella* (gestures to picture poster for *U* and the pictured umbrella).

MICHAEL: *Uh* (also looking at the poster).

MRS. EDDEY: That's the *U* (sound).

The focus in this quick conference could have been on all of the sounds in *jungle*, but the decision was to reinforce one sound. These *help conferences* serve to advance the learner's knowledge of encoding by providing a scaffold for phonics use during the drafting process.

Revision Conferences   *Revision conferences* are usually about meaning issues in children's drafts, but primary grade writers often need both meaning and encoding support. Many of the drafts of young writers take place in the child's imagination more than on the paper. Conferences work back and forth between the writer's intended meaning and the task of encoding.

Darren's letter to Michael Jordan involves a partial text. He is still trying to decide on the meaning. The conference begins with Darren reading his letter. *Dear Michael Jordan, I like your dunk. I like-*

DARREN: I like your (thinks for a moment about his topic) . . .

MRS. EDDEY: (reads the repeated phrase to prompt new ideas) I like your (pauses) what else do you like about Michael Jordan?

DARREN: Like (sighs) the basketball hoop is over here and he . . .

MRS. EDDEY: his shooting?

DARREN: (continues) He goes from way over here, and he's shooting.

MRS. EDDEY: (pausing between each word) I like your shooting. Let's try *shooting. sh*

DARREN: *S H*

MRS. EDDEY: You've got it, *sh-OO* (emphasizes the *oo* sound). As Darren writes *O T,* she adds a second O and pronounces the word). *Shoot ing* Do you know what letters spell *-ing?*

DARREN: (Makes a face to show his disinterest).

MRS. EDDEY: O.K., *I like your shooting (pauses) from far . . .*

DARREN: (very excited) from far *R* (writing as he talks) *F O M*

MRS. EDDEY: From far away. (She starts to say *away* slowly.) It's kind of hard to hear. *a-w-a* (Darren writes *A*). What letter does *way* start with?

DARREN: (Goes to the chart to look at letters, returns and writes *W* and another *A*.)

MRS. EDDEY: Almost, (continuing on) I like your—

DARREN: Picture.

MRS. EDDEY: (Writes the word *picture*.) I'm going to write some words here and you can use them as you write. (Writes *shooting, from, far,* and *away* in a box at the side.)

Clearly, Mrs. Eddey picked her battles in terms of which sounds the student could represent and which might be left for another day. The scaffold she provided emphasized listening to sounds in words and using available information (the letter from the chart, known letter-sound relationships, and the words written in the box). She did not interrupt the emerging text ideas with elaborate instruction about particular sounds.

Editing Conferences *Editing conferences* help move a draft to its final form. The teacher and student can talk about various word attempts, correct punctuation, and look at spacing as well as other surface text matters. With an emphasis on correcting attempted words, there are often rich opportunities for phonics instruction in these more lengthy conferences. Drafts that are not being published do not have to be corrected down to the last word. There are a number of options a teacher may choose:

- Focus on letter-sound relations of key words in the draft. These are the words that are essential.

- Talk about a specific phonics pattern that occurs in several words. Circle all the words showing that pattern and correct one or two in the conference, asking the child to correct the rest independently.

- Select encoding issues that are related to recent phonics mini-lessons. Reinforce that instruction and identify words that fit the pattern.

In thinking through each editing conference, teachers consider what they know about an individual learner's letter-sound knowledge, the opportunities for instruction in the current draft, and recent classroom instruction within the writing program. Taking these into account, the editing conference is an occasion where teachers conduct tailor-made instruction for each learner.

An example of this decision making can be seen in Mrs. Eddey's editing conference with Nina, a first-grade writer who needs extensive support with encoding.

NINA HAS WRITTEN:	CONVENTIONAL SPELLING:
I get Hrt.	I got hurt.
My sist Ras me.	My sister scratches me.
Vats hi I get hrt.	That's how I got hurt.
She dtan wot to play wa me.	She didn't want to play with me.
She mat me mat.	She makes me mad.

Nina's draft shows that she uses writing to say something she cares about. Her writing has voice and clearly expressed ideas. Nina knows the conventional spelling of some words (*she, me, I, my, to,* and *play*) and makes attempts at others. She represents every word she needs. The teacher could work on improving the spelling attempts that Nina makes, focusing on every word that does not have a conventional spelling, or, since this piece is not being published, simply choose some of the words that are particularly important to correct.

DECISION: Emphasize hearing sounds in words. Provide a scaffold for correcting vowel sounds, since they have been emphasized in writing class.

MRS. EDDEY: Let's go back and work on some of the sounds we hear in some of the words. You did a good job here on *I got hurt*. Now look at the letter you put in the middle of this word (gestures to *get*). If I'm going to read this word I'm going to say *g-e-t*, but you read *got*, so what vowel would you put here in the middle?

NINA: O

MRS. EDDEY: (reading on) I got hurt, my sis-ter. Let's see what other sounds we hear. You got the first three sounds very nicely. (She stretches out the sounds.)

The conference continues with Mrs. Eddey providing a scaffold for encoding as Nina represents the sounds in *scratched, that's, didn't, want, makes,* and *mad*. At the end of the conference, just after Nina sounds out *mad*, they talk about how to work independently.

Mrs. Eddey: Why is it that I see so many of these words that don't have [all] the sounds in them? Are you saying the words to yourself as you're writing them? Do they look right to you when you've finished writing them? You can try a second time [if you're in doubt] because every time you did a second time, you did it almost perfectly. Now I want you to start working on the words yourself.

The teacher's talk in this conference keeps Nina's attention directed appropriately and serves as a model for how to work out more conventional spellings. This editing conference met three important purposes:

- Showed how to represent sounds needed in specific key words.
- Moved the writer along developmentally.
- Summarized what the learner needed to do independently.

Summary of Phonics Support in Writing Workshop

Writing workshop programs provide opportunities to emphasize phonics concepts as children write and edit their work. The teacher has a number of options.

- Develop minilessons to address encoding problems that appear in the writing of several students.
- Conference with children about the words they need to spell during drafting.
- Show children how to connect the particular concepts addressed in phonics instruction with their own writing efforts.
- Conduct editing conferences that address encoding problems.

JANICE EDDEY:
TEACHER TO TEACHER

My writing workshop program is driven by the children's own topics and by giving them time each day to work as writers. There is a strong emphasis on the public sharing of their pieces. Children tell back what they hear and ask the author questions such as: "I don't understand that part," or "Did you put all your sounds in the words?" The writing community helps encourage children to attempt more and to move forward both in conventions as well as craft. We celebrate published pieces in our writing community. I believe in a balance of doing things—practicing it (as they do when they work on their own pieces) and then a time to share. I truly feel that children need authentic audiences for whatever they do. They need real purposes for their writing.

Each class has its own personality. The class this year has an emphasis on personal communication; notes between people and letters to authors. When the responses come back, they are even more interested. Other years children are motivated by nonfiction, doing research, and writing about what they learn. Children seem to develop a genre that they most enjoy writing in. Being in an urban school, writing workshop becomes their voice—their favorite part of the day.

I try to think about the needs of children. My minilessons in writing workshop sometimes come from their own writing. I look at what they're doing in their writing and then I plan my minilesson based on the needs that I see. Each week I try to cover craft, procedures, and phonics in the minilessons. I also think there has to be a combination of whole group, small group, and individual instruction in a program like this. Basically, the small group work I do is more skill-oriented; large group is for general concept work, and individual conferences are when I really focus on the individual needs of a particular child and come as close as I possibly can to meeting those needs.

In my writing program there's a place for children to sign-up for help, revision support, and editing. After the room gets settled and everyone is writing, I go to the people who signed up and work with them. At the back table I do the editing conferences. I basically work with words written in their first try. I help the child make a second attempt and see if together we can get closer to the letters and sounds needed. I also try to help them decide if they have more to write about the topic.

There are other supports for learning phonics. We do a home newsletter using interactive writing and study word patterns in spelling. Children read independently and read in groups, and often there is writing as part of those reading experiences. We have an elaborate literature program here. As a school we have literature themes and they include author visits. Our themes are woven into the stories I read to the class and are featured in the book collection. Children read every day from real books and many times these books are motivation for children to attempt different types of writing.

I have a philosophy. I really think what I do in teaching about phonics is to talk about basic concepts, show some strategies, and then give children lots of time to practice in writing workshop. Then I reinforce what I see the child doing during the editing conference. I choose one phonics skill to practice during our conference.

During sharing I like to have a range of children in a group so they can learn from each other. They listen to other children's writing and share ideas with their friends. They make individual breakthroughs when they've tried the new idea or letter-sound concept for themselves. That's what happens when they write every day. Through writing, children develop lots of confidence in letter-sound relationships and develop into authors. Then writing gives them a connection with the books they read.

9

Writing to Share the Pen and Phonics Knowledge

In January, the children arrive at the classroom very excited about the first snowfall of the season. Jo Anne Abreu gathers them around her and invites them to tell about their adventures in the snow. Next, she suggests they write sentences together. Anne volunteers, "I can make a snow person."

MRS. ABREU: All right, I need help spelling *can*. That's a word I think you know.

ANNE: *C A N.*

MRS. ABREU: (Writes *can.*) *Can.* Look at that closely, boys and girls. That's the word *can*. Rhymes with *pan* and *man*. Now, we want the word *make. m-a-k-e.* Michael, let's try *make.*

MICHAEL: *M A* (Teacher writes *MA.*)

MRS. ABREU: *kk*

MICHAEL: *C*

MRS. ABREU: Could be a *C* but it's a (pause)

MICHAEL: *K*

MRS. ABREU: Look at this closely, Michael (pointing to the written text *mak*). When you read this word in books, it needs something else. It doesn't look right to my eyes. It needs another vowel. It needs the vowel *E.* (She adds the *E* to *mak.*)

After children generate several sentences, they read through the sentences together. Mrs. Abreu introduces the big book version of Ezra Jack Keat's *The Snowy Day* (1962). A shared reading of the book extends the talk about possibilities for activities in the snow.

In this example, the teacher builds on the knowledge students have about the sounds represented by letters in their names. She uses everything the children appeared to know at the time of the lesson and then, through demonstration and explanation, extends their knowledge by providing the letters representing unfamiliar sounds. The children are excited about their adventures in the snow. Writing about them is a natural and meaningful activity.

Teachers use writing demonstrations to show the skills and strategies good writers use as they write. At times, they write for children, with the teacher doing all of the writing and thinking aloud as she writes, sharing her decisions. Other times, they write with children, sharing the pen and actively involving the children in collaborating to construct the text.

In this chapter we show ways teachers teach phonics within whole group writing contexts, including shared writing, interactive writing, and writing demonstrations. Although similar in nature, these approaches differ in the level of support provided by the teacher, the level of participation by students, and the focus for writing. In shared writing, the teacher holds the pen and does all of the writing. It is a collaborative writing event, with the children and teacher negotiating the text. In interactive writing, the pen is shared between the teacher and the students as they write collaboratively. Writing demonstrations often include both shared writing and interactive writing. These are elaborate writing events with the primary focus on the author's craft.

Contexts for Whole Group Writing

Children's literature selections, the children's everyday experiences, and the teacher's personal writing provide contexts for whole group writing. Teachers talk about how texts are put together—how stories work or how one looks for information in expository texts and records information—and what good writers do when they write. These contexts serve as scaffolds for the development and integration of the language processes—listening, speaking, reading, and writing—and for authentic skill and strategy instruction.

Children's Literature

Read alouds of trade books from various genres provide the framework or springboard for writing extensions. For example, following several readings of *Alexander and the Wind-Up Mouse* (Lionni, 1969), Mrs. Abreu involves the children in an oral retelling of the story. This leads to the children's collaboratively written retelling. The repeated readings help the children reconstruct the story line, recall characters, and remember the information necessary to generate a retelling, and ultimately construct the written text.

Children's Experiences

Like the scene described at the beginning of this chapter, events experienced by the children often provide the focus for whole group writing. For example, following a visit by a parent and her drama troupe, a shared writing in Mrs. Dapoz's classroom focused on composing a thank-you note.

Mrs. Dapoz: Before Mrs. Flessinger gets here, we need to do a thank-you that she can share with her actors. Who knows how to spell *dear*?

Jamie: *D E A R* or the real *deer*?

Allison: It's a homophone!

Mrs. Dapoz: (Writes *dear*.) How do you spell *Mrs.*?

Randy: *M R S*

Mrs. Dapoz: *Flessinger*—that's a long last name. Sometimes when you guys are writing you say, "That word is too long. I can't figure it out." Sometimes we can figure out long spellings if we work on them short parts at a time. What are the first two letters of her name?

Allison: *F L*

Mrs. Dapoz: Very good. *F-l-e-ss*

Mark: *E*

Mrs. Dapoz: *E*, good. (Writes *E*.) *Fl-e-S*

Randy: *S*

Mrs. Dapoz: Randy, good thinking today. Are there two *Ss* in her name? (Writes *SS*.) OK, you all know this, *–ing*.

Children: *I N G*

Mrs. Dapoz: A lot of you know this, too. *er*?

Children: *E R*

Mrs. Dapoz: When you end a word, it's never like *R*, but sometimes *ER*. What goes here?

Tim: comma.

Mrs. Dapoz: Look, you spelled the whole word.

In this example, Mrs. Dapoz assists the children in spelling the parent's last name by applying the strategy of stretching out a long word to listen for individual letter sounds and familiar chunks.

Teacher's Personal Stories

At times it is the teacher's personal stories that become the context for a writing demonstration. With children seated around her, Mrs. Abreu composes her stories in front of them, making explicit what she is doing. As she writes, she talks about her thinking, the decisions she is making as a writer, such as format, vocabulary, spelling, and punctuation. The children observe the process and are invited to help. In the scene that follows, Mrs. Abreu composes a story about her cat. The class is currently working on a unit about pets.

The writing demonstration begins with a shared reading of the big book, *Cookie's Week* (Ward, 1988), a story about a cat. This leads to a brief discussion about experiences with pets. Using this discussion as a springboard for writing, Mrs. Abreu steps to the easel and writes a short story about her cat, Fluffy. As she writes, she talks about the decisions she is making as a writer and invites children to help her.

MRS. ABREU: I'm going to write about my pet, Fluffy. She's a cat and we call her Fluffy because she is big and furry. So I'm going to begin my story with a sentence, *My cat is big and furry*.

Mrs. Abreu talks about each word as she writes it, involving the children in decisions about letter choices and elongating the sounds as she writes and says the words *b-i-g, a-n-d*.

MRS. ABREU: *furry*. What sounds do you hear in *furry*?

ERIN: *E*

MRS. ABREU: Yes, I hear *E*, too. Where do you hear it?

ERIN: At the end.

MRS. ABREU: What other sounds do you hear in *furry*? I'm going to write *furry*.

(She stretches out the sounds as she writes *furry*.)

MRS. ABREU: (running her finger under the word, left-to-right) *furry*. I hear *E* but there's not an *E* in *furry*. What letter is making the *E* sound?

CHILDREN: *Y*

Mrs. Abreu continues her story, sharing her thinking as she writes and actively involving the children in spellings of words, decisions for choice of vocabulary, and rereadings of the story.

Following the demonstration, the children go back to their desks to write. They may write about their own pets or about any topic of their choice. Mrs. Abreu circulates through the room, assisting individual children as needed.

Mrs. Abreu explains:

I demonstrate how to write. I write in front of them and talk out loud while I'm writing so they can see what's in my head as a writer. The children help me with some of the spelling and some of the words.

Skills and Strategies Taught in Context

Skills and strategies are embedded within whole group writing events. Each event requires different levels of teacher support appropriate to each child's level of development. Early in the year, teachers attend more to conventions of print, such as moving from left-to-right, spacing between words, punctuation, and beginning letter-sound relationships. Later in the year, the children are familiar with the routine and much more sophisticated in their knowledge about the conventions of print. They are able to hear the sounds in words, sequence the sounds they hear, represent them with letters, and discern many different patterns. The children are also aware that their purpose for writing dictates the type of writing they undertake.

The Structure of a Writing Demonstration

A writing demonstration is organized into three connected parts:

- establish a context and a framework for writing;
- compose the text;
- make a transition to independent writing.

During the actual composing, the focus is on constructing a meaningful text while using problem-solving strategies to figure out the spellings of unknown words. The teacher and the children discuss what to write and, at times, share the pen with the teacher assisting students *as needed*. The teacher keeps in mind what the child understands about how written language works and what the next instructional step should be. See Chapter Two on Assessment to learn how teachers gather information about their students and decide what to teach.

The third part of the demonstration serves as closure and a transition to independent work in the writing workshop. Students can follow the demonstration or they can write on a topic of their own choice. Mrs. Abreu explains: "I usually say, 'If you came to school today with a story in your head and you need to get it down on paper, you are welcome to do that, as long as you are writing.'"

Meeting Individual Needs in Whole Group Writing

Whole group writing is a collaborative event. Everyone has a role and is expected to participate. To support young writers and to encourage active participation, teachers vary the writing approaches between shared writing and interactive writing. These shifts are responsive to children's levels of performance. When individual children come to the chart to write, the teacher supports that child precisely at the point of need. This is the case, for example, as Mrs. Abreu assists Elsie (a child with Down Syndrome included in this classroom) to write the phrase *in Annie's room*. Mrs. Abreu explains:

> I knew she [Elsie] can spell *in*, so I brought her up to write *in*.
> But I knew *Annie's room* would be difficult for her, so I let her

write the capital *A* and the two *N*s, which she knows, and I helped her with the rest of the word. If I only called on children at the point where they are [knowledgeable] developmentally, I would lose most of them. They have to own the process.

Thus, writing demonstrations do not follow a predictable sequence beginning with shared writing and moving to interactive writing, but evolve in various ways:

- teacher understanding of composing;
- teacher sensitivity to students' needs;
- and student's willingness to take a risk.

Shifts also occur when writing becomes tedious or a needed word is too difficult for the individual child or group to attempt. At these times, teachers take the pen and write aloud to speed the process.

A Close-up Look at One Writing Demonstration

We take a close-up look at one writing demonstration as it occurs in Mrs. Abreu's classroom. Throughout the demonstration, teacher moves will be shown to emphasize decision making.

The following letter-writing activity about an imaginary trip to the Planet C-Wetss is embedded in a classroom theme of Space. Class members take the role of Gunk, an alien, writing to Jason on Earth. The demonstration begins with a shared reading of a large letter displayed on an easel that Mrs. Abreu has written to the class.

> Dear Class,
>
> Today is Monday, the 159th day of first grade. We have learned about our solar system by reading books. Can you find some facts about Saturn for me? Please write back and tell me what you know about Saturn.
>
> Sincerely,
> Mrs. Abreu

The children respond to her question in writing as part of their morning seatwork and later share facts about Saturn from their writing. After listening to three or four letters, Mrs. Abreu thanks the volunteers and moves to the big book, *Somewhere in the Universe* (Drew, 1988) for a shared reading. She then moves to the easel nearby.

MRS. ABREU: Now, we're going to write a letter to Jason [a character in the book] and we're going to address the envelope. So, the first thing we need to do, we need to write Jason's name down. (She places a large envelope on the easel.)

> **DECISION**: Say the word slowly, stretching out the sounds to help the children hear the individual phonemes.

MRS. ABREU: *J-a-s-o-n*. (Many hands go up. She points to a child. The child comes to the chart and writes *JASEN*.)

> **DECISION**: Slide finger under the individual letters to encourage one-to-one matching of letters and sounds.

MRS. ABREU: O.K., let's check it. *J-A-S-E-N*. This is a good guess (pointing to the *E*), but we need an *O* here (she writes *O* over the *E*). *JasON* (emphasizing the *on* sound) like [the word] *ON* that we see on the word wall.

Together, Mrs. Abreu and the children address the envelope. Mrs. Abreu shares the pen with the children during writing. They give Jason a last name, and write his street address, city, state, country, planet. Jointly, Mrs. Abreu and the children then compose a letter from Gunk to Jason. The task is for Gunk to give Jason information about Planet C-Wetss and to ask a question.

MRS. ABREU: Let's write to Jason. Now, Gunk is an alien. Remember when the person from Planet X came? What did the person from Planet X find out when he came down here? We just read the story today. Let's go back to Mrs. Abreu's letter and see how it started.

> **DECISION**: Draw upon shared reading to establish a framework for writing. Refer to the morning letter as a model.

MRS. ABREU: How did I start it?

PAULA: *dear*.

MRS. ABREU: Doug, go up and write *dear*.

Doug begins writing *DER*, hesitates, and then changes the *R* to an *A*.

MRS. ABREU: Look what Doug did. He started *D E R* and right away he realized what, Doug?

DOUG: I left out the *A*.

MRS. ABREU: Do [other] writers ever do that? Do I ever do that?

CHILDREN: Yes.

MRS. ABREU: He knew right away and he just turned the *R* into an *A*. Seeing it on paper, you realized you had skipped a letter. It didn't look right to your eyes.

> **DECISION**: Talk about the strategy Doug used. He rechecked his writing by rereading to see if it looked right.

With Mrs. Abreu's help, Doug finishes writing the salutation, *DEAR JASON*. Again, Mrs. Abreu refers back to her morning letter. Since her letter began by giving information, she suggests the letter from Gunk follow the same format.

MRS. ABREU: What is Gunk going to tell Jason about his planet, C-Wetss?

ANNA: Everybody here owns 12,000 cats.

MRS. ABREU: Of course. Very good! Writers always write what they know about. Anna always writes what she knows about. Now I'm beginning to know something about C-Wetss.

Mrs. Abreu hands the pen to Adrian to write *everybody*. Adrian steps to the easel. She looks at Mrs. Abreu.

MRS. ABREU: Is *everybody* on the word wall?

CHILDREN: No.

MRS. ABREU: No, but *everywhere* is. Ruth, spell *every* for her.

RUTH: *E V E R Y.*

Adrian writes *every*.

MRS. ABREU: Ruth, what word is on the word wall?

RITH: *everywhere.*

MRS. ABREU: And, we want to write *everyBODY*. It's a compound word. She sounds out the word and emphasizes vowel sounds as they occur. She talks about the short *O* sound and refers to the class poster of an *octopus*. The writing continues.

> **DECISION**: Stretch out the sounds to hear the individual phonemes in the word.

Mrs. Abreu: *Everybody here* owns *o-w-n-s* _____ that's not on the Word Wall. What do you hear?

Child: *O* [long *o*]

> **DECISION**: Look at O-Man the Snowman chart. (Words with different spellings for long *o* are listed on the snowman). Children are familiar with the patterns.

MRS. ABREU: Does anybody know what comes after *O* in *owns*? (looking around the room).

MICHAEL: *O W*

MRS. ABREU: You're right. *OW* is right so far. *owN owN*

MICHAEL: *N*

MRS. ABREU: *everybody here ownS.*

The writing continues. Later the group is working on the sentence: *Star Wars and beanie babies are popular.* Mrs. Abreu assists Alex as he writes the word *popular.*

MRS. ABREU: *pop*

ALEX: *P O P*

MRS. ABREU: *u* (long *U* sound) *pop-U-lar* What comes next?

ALEX: *U*

MRS. ABREU: Yes. Now, *lar*

ALEX: *L*

MRS. ABREU: Now, what letter comes after the vowel? What's the last letter going to be in *popular?*

ALEX: *R*

MRS. ABREU: So, now we have to decide on the vowel?

ALEX: *E*

MRS. ABREU: Take another guess. This is what happens with "Bossy R," Alex. We have to make guesses sometimes. *populAR. cAR.* Want to try one more guess? You already said *E*, so . . .

ALEX: *U*

Alex continues to guess until he guesses *A.*

DECISIONS: Use analogy. Keep substituting vowels. Visually the word may look right to Alex when his guess is right.

Many more decisions are negotiated regarding time, message, questions to ask, and spellings. Mrs. Abreu continually reminds children of the context, purpose, and audience. Often, they return to her letter to the class as a model, scaffolding the teaching and learning event. When completed, Mrs. Abreu and the children read through the letter together, pointing to the words and checking for meaning. They decide it is ready for the Galaxy Mail Service.

Dear Jason,

Everybody here owns 12,000 cats. Star Wars and Beanie Babies are popular. Would you like for me to bring you one of my cats?

From,

Gunk

Mrs. Abreu closes the demonstration with directions for writing workshop.

MRS. ABREU: This is writing workshop. You're going to write in your journals today and I want it to have something to do with Space. It can be nonfiction where you're writing facts or you can write about an alien and the name you want to give him or her, but it has to have something to do with Space.

CHILD: Can it be a poem?

MRS. ABREU: It can be a poem. Oh, I'd love to hear a poem!

The children return to their desks and begin writing. Mrs. Abreu moves around the room assisting children as needed.

This writing demonstration as a whole includes:

- a demonstration of what good writers do when they write (thinking about purpose and audience)
- a demonstration of letter writing (format)
- a demonstration of strategies used to spell words (phonemic segmentation, analogy, classroom environment)

In summary, whole group writing provides supportive and authentic frameworks for instruction in phonics skills and strategies within meaningful contexts. As texts are jointly constructed, teachers demonstrate a network of strategies that encourage their students to attend to information from different sources. Students learn the conventions of spelling, syntax, and meaning as they engage in these lessons. They also learn about writer's craft—what good writers do when they write—as they interact with more knowledgeable writers. The organization of these events assists participants as they try to connect and organize their thinking about literacy.

JO ANN ABREU:
TEACHER TO TEACHER

Writing demonstrations begin day one in my first-grade class. The children need these demonstrations. They need to hear the thought processes; what good writers do when they write. They need to see me as a writer. They need to see me go through the process and do it in front of them. Sometimes, the children help me with my own personal story, or we write a story together extending children's literature or their own experiences.

Writing demonstrations are active. I'm not just sitting on a chair directing. I'm up. I'm moving to the word wall to demonstrate using the room or sending someone to the word wall to check out the spelling of a word. My body is involved in it, my voice is involved in it, the children are involved in it. We talk a lot. We use language to problemsolve. We talk about format, sentence structure, choice of words, how to spell a word, etc. I encourage them to use the room—word family charts, stories written previously and on display, books on the chalk ledge. Once we do some sort of writing together, I hang it up in the room. I think it's important for them to see me do this, so they know where to look for it to get help.

Writing demonstrations are preplanned. I have a product in mind. I know where I want the children to go as writers, what their needs are, and what they're ready for. But the process, once underway, often changes. I never know exactly where the children are going to lead me. I need to be flexible. The children have to have some ownership in what they're doing, and I'm constantly looking at their needs. I constantly tie into literature. We talk about authors and books and how authors create their stories. I always put them in the author's shoes, first as a reader and then as a writer.

Although I don't plan writing demonstrations to teach phonics necessarily, phonics does happen throughout. It's difficult to write without dealing with the sounds and patterns of the language. When a child comes up and needs help spelling a word, they sometimes call on someone else for help. Or, usually, I prompt them, saying, "What's that sound? Can you think of another word that has that sound?" Sometimes we have to make corrections or fix things. But then, we get right back to the story. I try teaching a point, just to take advantage of the moment, but then we go back to the main focus of the activity—writing a meaningful piece.

I'm a strong believer in building community. The children have to feel emotionally safe and able to take risks. They need to feel good about themselves, and then learning can take place. We have many celebrations, such as when a child spells a word such as *was* or *is*. I say, "Wow! You spelled that right. You own that word. You'll be spelling that word right for the rest of your life, because you own it." This gives them pride. We talk about how not everyone is in the same place at the same time, and that's O.K. We respect that. So, my writing demonstrations are about: Where can I take them today? What new places can we explore? What can we do today that they will be able to use when they go back to their seats and make some kind of connection? and What can I add to what I did yesterday? Really, it all comes down to the children and their needs and making decisions based on those needs.

10 Project Work: Learn Phonics While Exploring the World

It's January and Tom is just beginning to understand how to represent the sounds in words with letters. He is an active, talkative boy who likes to listen to tapes, play, and tease. Beth Swanson knows Tom has not been very interested in reading or writing, but he has enjoyed painting a large, colorful mural as part of a unit on homes. He and Mrs. Swanson now sit side-by-side at a student table working to create labels for his artwork before it goes on display.

MRS. SWANSON: What labels do you want?

TOM: *chimney*. (He offers the first word he wants to write.)

MRS. SWANSON: What two letters start that one . . . like *children* (meaning *chimney* and *children* have the same initial letters).

TOM: *ch*

MRS. SWANSON: What letters [represent that sound]?

TOM: *H*

MRS. SWANSON: (Writes a short blank line followed by *H*.) *H* is one of the letters. Do you know *chugga, chugga, choo choo*? (The teacher refers to a book on tape the children listen to.) Do you know the other letter?

TOM: *H*

MRS. SWANSON: We have that. (She points to the *H* already on the paper.)

TOM: *P*

MRS. SWANSON: It's *C*. (Student writes *C*.) What's the word? (Points to the label, trying to get him to remember and pronounce the word they are trying to write.)

Tom shrugs.

MRS. SWANSON: It's *chimney*. What do you hear? (Asking what letter sounds he hears in the word.)

Tom: *M*

Mrs. Swanson: (She writes *MN* after the *H*. She offers the pencil to the child.) You write. It's a vowel [the next letter they are looking for]. Do you know the vowels?

Tom shrugs and sets the pencil down.

Mrs. Swanson: *A, E, I, O, U* like the tape. Do you know the tape? (She refers to a tape about vowels the students listen to.)

Tom does not respond.

Mrs. Swanson: It ends *E Y.* (She writes *E Y.*)

Tom cuts the label off the strip of paper and glues it on the mural.

Mrs. Swanson: What word is it? (Points to the label.)

Tom: *Chimney.*

Mrs. Swanson: (nodding) What do you want next?

They continue for several more minutes in this pattern. Through careful questioning, Mrs. Swanson guides his creation of labels that say *pumpkins, clouds,* and *snowflakes* for the mural. This is a long time for Tom to sit and focus on writing.

Decision: Use Tom's interest in his mural to motivate him to write. Help him make connections so he can apply the things he knows.

Project work consists of in-depth explorations. This investigative research can be the approach for the majority of teaching and learning in a class, or project work can support, supplement, and integrate more direct instruction.

Advantages and Benefits of Project Work

Project work provides the active, hands-on, holistic learning that is developmentally appropriate for young students. Young children don't see the distinct knowledge domains we have created. They look for answers to their questions and naturally integrate reading, writing, math, social studies, and science. This cross-disciplinary approach encourages children to grow intellectually as they make connections within and between these domains. The cooperative learning inherent in project work helps children develop their abilities to work with others. All students, including children with special needs, can build on their personal backgrounds, interests, needs, and strengths.

Through projects, children become accountable for pursuing their own learning. They choose the aspects of the topic they want to follow and define their questions. They decide the best way to find the answers to those questions and they select the type of product that will best present what they have learned. These choices and their personal contribution to the learning process help motivate students and capitalize on children's natural curiosity and social nature. The students are active investigative reporters of knowledge.

Finally, project work encourages children to use higher level thinking skills. While searching for answers, they first locate information, then analyze and synthesize it. The information becomes their own as they represent it in various forms to share with the rest of the class. During sharing, the listeners can learn from their peers and vicariously experience other ways of learning. All the students can reflect on their new knowledge and can evaluate their processes, thinking about the learning modes that work well for them and those that do not. Researching a topic requires using knowledge learned previously and applying literacy skills. Project work leads children to see the purpose and importance of basic reading, writing, and mathematical skills they are working to learn at school. The next section of this chapter reviews the development of a project, followed by examples of project work that show students extending their current literacy development, including phonics.

Development of a Project

We can visualize the flow of project work as an hourglass shape: wide, narrow, then wide again. The topic of the unit of study is broad, like the top of an hourglass. The students discuss what they already know about the topic. They then brainstorm what they would like to know more about. They create questions about those aspects of the unit topic. This process is explained in detail in the following section **Choose, Recall, and Wonder**. The middle of the hourglass is narrow. There isn't time for everyone to investigate every single aspect of the topic. Individuals or small groups of students choose certain focus questions about the topic. They search in a variety of ways (observe, interview, read, etc.) for information to answer those questions. In preparation for communicating it to the rest of the class, they depict the discovered information in the form of a product. The second section, **Focus, Research, and Represent**, describes this part of the process. The bottom of the hourglass is wide again. The third section, **Report, Connect, and Reflect**, recounts how to bring all the narrow focus questions and their answers together again. The students share their products. The whole class talks about connections among the answers to the focus questions. The teacher helps the children link the new information to what was previously known to assemble a broader understanding of the topic of the unit.

Before project work can begin, the children need to understand what a project is and what it is not. Some students have done projects before, but most will need a great deal of experience before they can do them independently. The teacher needs to demonstrate different ways to choose a topic, explore it, record information, report, and reflect. The teacher's role in project work is that of a consultant and supervisor, providing a productive work environment and monitoring student work. At Highland Park School, Mrs. Hootman and Mrs. Swanson use project work as an important part of their units. They schedule large blocks of work time in the morning and afternoon. Their students first complete required daily work, then proceed to continuing project work.

Choose, Recall, and Wonder: Curiosity Claimed the Class

The topic for the project work unit can come from the children or the teacher. The teacher can learn what interests the students by watching them work and play, and by listening to them talk. The students and their families can fill out interest surveys. The teacher may lead a class discussion asking the students to suggest possible topics. After a few ideas are written on the chalkboard, the students can brainstorm these potential topics, exploring their possibilities for project work. With experience in project work, the students will improve in their ability to suggest topics. Good project topics are about someone or something in the children's everyday experience that they can investigate. After the topic is decided, the teacher can use a visual organizer like a web or filling the first two sections of a KWL chart (What do we KNOW? What do we WANT to know? What have we LEARNED?) to help the children see their ideas and create questions to answer about various aspects of the topic. (The third section will be filled out at the end of the project.)

The best way to learn how to do project work is to experience it. Teachers may choose to have their class do initial project work together as a whole group. Mrs. Swanson and Mrs. Hootman guide their children closely during the first project of the year. The children work on a topic about something meaningful to them: themselves! By starting with a simple topic that is interesting to all, easily understood, and with many readily available sources of information, the students can concentrate on learning the process. The students can choose which aspect about themselves they would like to focus on. The focus may be a vacation, a favorite book, a movie, or a television show. The students are encouraged to share whatever interests them, but they must follow the school rule to avoid violence and weapons, which sometimes requires discussion about a movie's or television show's focus. Later in the school year, after the class has worked through several units, Mrs. Hootman and Mrs. Swanson encourage the students to generate ideas for study such as *dinosaurs* or *nighttime*. These topics are put to a class vote. After a topic is selected, the students then choose which aspects they want to explore, who to work with, where to sit, and how they would like to express their learning.

Focus, Research, and Represent: Divide and Conquer

After the class has decided on a topic and possible questions they want to answer, the students can work more independently. They may work alone, with a partner, or in a small group, depending on which focus questions interest them. Some projects lend themselves more readily to group work. Questions of wide appeal may bring several interested students together. Inquiry that entails quite a bit of work may require several workers to share the task. Group work requires children to negotiate the roles and responsibilities of the members. (Who will find which books? Who will keep track of the information they discover? Later, who will bring the required paper towel tubes to create the product?) Mrs. Swanson and Mrs. Hootman have found through experience that their first graders work best in groups of no more than three children.

Depending on the topic, available resources, and personal preference, the students research the topic in a variety of ways. They may investigate through direct observation during field trips (inside the building and beyond), listening to speakers, interviewing, surveying, reading related books, looking at photographs and videotapes, experimenting, collecting items, etc. The goal is to figure out the best way to find the information to answer the focus question(s).

Final products are used to represent information for sharing. The students contemplate what they have learned while they create products. The information acquired guides the product choice and the materials used to create it. For example, the results of a survey on preferred school lunch might be presented in a graph, whereas the results of reading library books on George Washington might be presented by a portrait with a speech bubble of interesting facts. Mrs. Swanson and Mrs. Hootman introduce product choices very slowly. They start with the simpler products, such as tallying the results of a survey of a few classmates, or writing in a wallpaper book. (Volunteers make their wallpaper books from several blank pieces of paper stapled between two pieces of wallpaper samples that form the cover.) Products later in the school year may be a play (with dialogue, costumes, and a mural backdrop) or a movie (cartoons drawn on shelf paper scrolled past a window cut in a box). The teachers often share examples of products created by former students, discussing how they were made and pointing out the important aspects. Step-by-step they demonstrate the procedure for making each product, sharing the thinking process, and discussing where the necessary supplies are located. It is December before all the choices are introduced. As they discuss and add different products to their repertoire, a piece of sentence strip paper listing that project is added to a metal ring. The teachers use this ring of choices when they talk about projects. The project ring is posted in the room, available to students who want to flip through the cards as they plan their work. Some of the products are simply writing pieces. Most of the choices build on young children's propensity to represent meaning with both art and writing.

PRODUCT IDEAS FOR THE PROJECT RING	
survey	diorama
wallpaper book	play
mural	science observation
puppet show	student's choice
mobile	collage
map	letter
song	sculpture
poem	picture book
newspaper	flag
game board	flip book
movie	

The students may want to draw, paint, or use other media to create their products. Children need access to a wide variety of materials to be free to create diverse products. The materials necessary for basic creations include various sizes and types of papers, pencils, markers, paints, brushes, shoeboxes, clay, flat wooden sticks for puppet holders, coat hangers for mobiles, etc. These resources must be stored in ways that are child-accessible. Mrs. Hootman and Mrs. Swanson give very specific guidelines for using materials appropriately. For example, they discuss pressing the lid on the marker until you hear the snap sound so the marker will not dry out. Painting is done in one location created by pushing several tables together and covering them. This area provides space for four students to paint on large paper at the same time. If the painting area is full, the other students do something else and wait for an opening.

Students may choose to alter or embellish a basic creation by adding detail. They may enhance 2-D art products with 3-D materials, and add labels or captions to art projects.

IDEAS FOR POSSIBLE ART EMBELLISHMENT MATERIALS		
feathers	sponge pieces	plastic grass
beads	ribbon	small pine cones
fringe	cloth pieces	dried flowers
lace	cardboard pieces	sand

fur	pompom balls	buttons
string, twine, yarn	cotton balls	paper cups
foil	toothpicks	pebbles
sequins	straws	seeds
flat wooden shapes	shells	styrofoam packing pieces

The attributes of the art materials suggest ways they can be used. Mrs. Swanson and Mrs. Hootman introduce each material and discuss how to best attach it to a product and what it might be used for. They demonstrate creating a product and thoughtfully choosing certain embellishments for specific reasons. For example, yarn is good to represent hair and cloth is good to represent a skirt in a portrait. They explain, "You don't just glue twenty pompoms on your mural because they are pretty. You have to have a reason to put it on. We often ask, 'Why did you chose to put it on there?'" Most of the children learn to use materials for an expressive purpose.

Report, Connect, and Reflect: What's It All About?

At this step in the development of a project, the attention shifts to visual and verbal reporting of findings as children share their work and stories. This stage completes the cycle of project work by bringing closure to *this* topic, but it also serves as a springboard to other topics. Although sharing occurs informally in the first two steps as students interact, a more formal sharing time provides a larger audience. The presenting students reflect on what they have learned. The audience students can learn about the topic and also get ideas on how other students investigate and record information. In the beginning of the year, the teachers demonstrate how to present products and writing to the group and how the audience is to respond. The students become more sophisticated in their presenting and responding skills as the year progresses. Their responses will evolve from "I like it" or "It's pretty" to "I like the bright colors you used. They make me feel happy" and "Using wooden sticks for handles on the puppets is a good idea."

After sharing aloud, the products are displayed to show the work is important and to motivate writing. Writing has an advantage over oral presentation because it allows visitors to learn about the products when the creators are not there to explain them. Class members and visitors from other classes read as much information as they are able. They may make comments or question the creator. Over time, the creators learn about the clarity of writing required for the audience to understand the text in their displays. These exhibits of learning, as well as discussions, photographs, and/or videotapes of the Focus, Research, and Represent stage, facilitate talking and thinking about what has been learned and how it was learned. When the displays come down to make room for new ones, the children decide if they want to take them home. When two or more children create one product, they need to figure out a fair distribution system, such as rolling dice to decide, alternating turns taking products home (suitable for frequent work partners), or, as a last resort, dividing the product, if possible.

Monitor, Assess, and Evaluate

Project work does not offer the obvious points of assessment of learning that workbook pages and chapter tests do. Teachers can, however, develop a system of assessing students at various stages. The students' progress through project work can be tracked on a class list with a place by each name to record dates and notes. The first entry may be records of the students reporting what they intend to do and how it fits in the unit of study. After receiving teacher approval to proceed, the students can be required to check in at various other points as needed. (For example, the students can report their decisions on the best ways to gather information, their intended products, genres of writing, etc.) As students become more proficient at project learning, they do not need such close supervision, but they still need to know they are responsible for their learning, and accountable for spending their time productively.

Most students do well when they focus on one project and complete it before starting another one. Sometimes younger students forget on Monday that they already started a project the week before! The teacher needs to monitor that they don't start multiple projects without finishing any of them. As students finish a product, the teacher may highlight their names on the class list to see at a glance whose work is still in progress. Younger students may spend a week on a project, while older students may be meaningfully engaged longer, and can record their own progress for teacher review.

Both the final product and the process of how the children work through the project can be assessed. Grading of products (writing and artwork) is done routinely in many classrooms, but some teachers are not accustomed to evaluating the learning process. It can be assessed through photographs, videotape, observation with anecdotal records or teacher-made checklists, interviews, or portfolio discussions. The teacher may want to make rubrics to explain the important aspects that will be considered and the criteria examined. The sample rubric in Table 10-1 is one possible example. The aspects to be assessed are listed in the first column. (Teachers will vary in which aspects they choose to assess.) Sample

TABLE 10-1   Project Assessment Rubric

	NEEDS IMPROVEMENT	GOOD	SUPERIOR
Focus selection	Even with teacher consultation, the student is unable to pick a focus related to the topic.	With teacher consultation, the student picks a focus related to the topic.	The student can pick a focus related to the topic without help.
	The focus is not meaningful to the student.	The focus is somewhat meaningful to the student.	The focus is very meaningful to the student.
Process	The student needs a great deal of teacher supervision to work through the project process.	The student works through the project with teacher supervision.	The student works through the project process independently.
	The student is usually off-task during project work time.	The student is rarely off-task during project work time.	The student is not off-task during project work time.
Collaboration	The student makes unproductive work partner choices.	The student makes acceptable work partner choices.	The student makes very productive work partner choices.
	The group members do not choose roles and responsibilities fairly and democratically.	The group members choose roles and responsibilities fairly and democratically with teacher supervision.	The group members independently chose roles and responsibilities fairly and democratically.

TABLE 10-1   (cont.)

	NEEDS IMPROVEMENT	GOOD	SUPERIOR
	All members of the group do not contribute to the group's success.	All members of the group contribute to the group's success.	All members of the group equitably contribute to the group's success.
	The group cannot settle disputes.	The group, with teacher supervision, settles disputes.	The group settles disputes independently.
Product— artwork	Is incomplete and/or lacks sufficient detail.	Is finished and has detail.	Is complete and has rich detail.
	Does not represent the information learned.	Represents the information learned.	Represents the information learned well.
	Is not created carefully in appropriate media.	Is created carefully in suitable media.	Is created with great care in appropriate media.
Product— writing	Is incomplete.	Is finished.	Is complete and well developed.
	Does not show the student is making progress in writing skills and strategies.	Shows the student is making some progress in writing skills and strategies.	Shows the student is making great progress in writing skills and strategies.
	Phonics learning is not evident.	Phonics learning is evident.	Advanced phonics learning is evident.

TABLE 10-1   (cont.)

	NEEDS IMPROVEMENT	GOOD	SUPERIOR
Sharing	The student does not prepare products for visual display. Even with a great deal of teacher support, the student cannot orally explain the process, artwork, and writing products.	The student prepares products for visual display. Supported by teacher questioning, the student orally explains the process, artwork, and writing products.	The student masterfully prepares products for visual display. Independently the student orally explains the process, artwork, and writing products well.

descriptions of three levels of achievement are in the row next to each aspect. If grades are desired, assessments by rubrics can be converted into grades by assigning benchmarks for grades. For example, a *superior* rating in at least five of the six areas may be an *A*, three ratings in *good* and three in *superior* may be a *B*, ratings averaging *good* may be a *C*, etc. Compiling the student's profile on the rubric will help the teacher see which parts of the project work process and products require more instruction for the students to be more productive. (See Chapter Two for an extended discussion of linking assessment with instruction.)

The Literacy Link

When students create products for project work, Mrs. Hootman and Mrs. Swanson expect every child to have some kind of writing to share with the class. Writing conferences provide the site for phonics instruction based on each child's writing. The writing generated in project work can be an important part of phonics teaching and learning. Regardless of the form it takes, such as labels for pictures, a sentence strip, a story or report, the invented spelling provides an excellent opportunity for the student to use the graphophonemic cueing system. The teacher guides the process with questions.

IDEAS FOR POSSIBLE WRITING

labels	newspaper articles
sentence captions	bumper sticker
speech bubbles	certificate
(like comic book captions)	letter
cheer	list
puppet show script	report
play script	text for a flip book or picture
movie script	picture book
chant or rap	story
various types of poems	student's choice
TV commercial script	

Creating Labels

Creating labels for artwork such as murals and dioramas is a common way to use literacy for meaningful purposes. The labels can be as simple as one word written on a piece of sentence strip paper. Labels are a good way for early writers to become engaged in the literacy connections of project work. Their brevity facilitates success when a writer is not yet ready to tackle the larger number of words and writing conventions required to create a sentence strip caption or narrative.

During a unit on the nursery rhyme "Hey, Diddle, Diddle," Mrs. Hootman works with a boy who needs a great deal of support to write labels for his mural. The following example comes from the second half of the school year when the students are accustomed to adding writing to their artwork and talking through the writing process with their teachers. Derrick, however, has just moved into the school district and joined the class. He does not appear very comfortable with writing. He is beginning to learn how to interact in a writing conference. Initially, he doesn't seem to understand this exchange is about writing. He participates as if they are having a discussion about the picture he has drawn until Mrs. Hootman uses specific questions to guide his thinking and responses.

MRS. HOOTMAN: Can you tell me what some of these things are? What's that a picture of? (Points to the large yellow blob.)

DERRICK: (Does not respond to question directly.) Yeah, but I didn't have room because it was too big. I messed up on the moon. Then I got it. It was a little bit more bigger.

MRS. HOOTMAN: O.K. Is that a picture of the moon?

DERRICK: Yeah, but I think it was the moon. But it needs to be a little bit more bigger.

MRS. HOOTMAN: O.K. We need to write *moon*. What do you think *moon* starts with? What letter?

DERRICK: *M?*

MRS. HOOTMAN: uh, huh. (She agrees. She writes *moon,* points to it, and looks at Derrick, meaning he should read it.)

DERRICK: *m-oo-n.*

MRS. HOOTMAN: What's that a picture of down there? (Points to a black blob.)

DERRICK: It's a picture of a cat.

MRS. HOOTMAN: O.K. What's *cat* going to start with? What letter do you think?

(She again segments the word, this time guiding Derrick to do the writing. Repeating this pattern of interaction, they proceed to label a hill and a rocket.)

This sample shows how a teacher can ask questions to guide a very early writer in the alphabetic principle. On his own, Derrick's writing has been scribbling. Mrs. Hootman shows him that he can represent the word he says with letters. She talks him through identifying the words he wants to write, saying the word out loud, and thinking of letters to represent the sounds he hears. She asks him to provide the initial letter in *moon*, then she supplies the rest of the word, acting as the scribe. She asks Derrick to identify and record the initial and final sounds in the word *cat*. She writes in the *A*, knowing that he is just beginning to record consonants, and is not ready for vowel sounds yet.

DECISION: Ask Derrick to identify and write some initial and final letters and provide the rest to help him be successful.

Sentence Strips

Following a read aloud of *Mary Wore a Red Dress and Henry Wore His Green Sneakers* by Merle Peek (1985), some of the students paint and decorate self-portraits. Many are paintings on large paper embellished with 3-D materials. They write sentences about their clothing on a paper sentence strip that will serve as a caption for the artwork. During conferences, the teachers ask many of the children to cut their sentence strips up into individual words and arrange them back into the sentence to practice the concept of word. They adjust their instruction for students who are in need of other support. One child can write the whole sentence unassisted, and understands the concept of word, so the teacher works on capitalization with him. Another boy has not yet figured out how to represent sounds with letters. Mrs. Swanson tells him, "What you say can be written and you write it in a certain way." The teacher demonstrates the process by writing his dictated sentence on the sentence strip. She then asks the child to trace over the word *red* with a red marker.

The following exchange is a section of a long writing conference with a student who wants to write, *Anna wore a feathery shirt all day long.* So far, the student has used several different sources of information to write, *Anna wore a feather.* She knows how to write her own name, *Anna.* She found *wore a* in the title on the cover of the book. She located *feather* on the label for the box that holds the feathers for artwork. She is now working on the last sound in *feathery.* Mrs. Swanson sits at a student worktable with Anna. Several children choose to sit at the table and work. They listen in on the conversation.

MRS. SWANSON: What comes at the end of *feathery?* It's kind of tricky.

ANNA: Letter *E.*

MRS. SWANSON: Think of a word like *Sally.* What's the last letter there?

SALLY: (She is sitting at the table.) It's a *Y.*

MRS. SWANSON: (She nods to confirm Sally's answer.) Sometimes *Y* sounds like an *E* and that's what this one is. Put a *Y* there (points to the end of the word *feather* on the paper).

Anna writes *Y* to finish *feathery.*

As the conference continues, Anna uses invented spelling for *dress.* She states that she knows the letters for the word *all* because those are her initials. Encouraged by the teacher to use the resources in the classroom, she finds the word *day* on the calendar. She uses invented spelling for *long.*

Although *feathery* is not a commonly used word, the teacher chooses to employ the child's oral language in her writing. Mrs. Swanson wants to show that she values what Anna says and wants Anna to see her own words in print without changing what she said. The teacher knows that Anna is just learning to hear and record the sounds in words. Mrs. Swanson supports this student using a variety of strategies to figure out how to represent the sounds she hears in the words that she wants for the caption. She helps Anna use several different resources (books, art supply box, calendar, and a classmate).

DECISION: Building on Anna's demonstrated ability to attend to the initial sounds in words, guide her to also listen to the final sounds in words. Encourage her to use many sources of information to become an independent learner.

Continuous Text

The following example is a small part of a much longer individual writing conference where the teacher supports the creation of text for a nocturnal project. Sam has written a story about a goblin. Mrs. Swanson asks him to read his story.

SAM: (Reads) I would hang him, up. I would chain him up. (The text is written: *I Woill ChrHa He Up. I Woill CraH HE up.*)

MRS. SWANSON: You read *I would hang him up. I would chain him up.* You have *chain* and *hang* with the same beginning sound. What do you think *hang* should start with?

SAM: *H*

MRS. SWANSON: Go ahead. (Sam understands this means he should change it, so he erases the *C* and writes *H* instead.)

Sam's writing shows he understands the concept of word and he has most of the initial consonants correct. He is starting to hear and record many letters beyond the initial sounds in words. She works with him on changing the only incorrect initial letter. She will wait and work on ending and middle sounds another day.

> **DECISION**: Guide Sam through a strategy of thoughtful crosschecking. Work on consistency of letter-sound relationships today and work on uppercase and lowercase letters later.

Conclusion

Teachers often plan units to fulfill required objectives in an interdisciplinary way by linking the teaching and learning of several subject areas. Teachers usually determine the sequence and scope of lessons, deciding the questions to be answered and the activities to be done. It takes a good deal of teacher work to create an exceptional unit. (No wonder teachers recycle some annually.) By contrast, project work involves the students in choice of topic, questions to be investigated, ways of learning, and modes of responding. Exploring a topic of interest and recording information are powerful reasons to use print. As they struggle to read or write about an interesting subject, children realize they need to know how to link the sounds and symbols of our language. In invented spelling, children have to figure out what letters are needed to spell the words they want to use to communicate. Phonics is essential to first record ideas in words (such as sentence strips, labels, or continuous text), then to read those words to classmates, and then to allow other people to read about the product later.

JENNY HOOTMAN AND BETH SWANSON: TEACHER TO TEACHER

This is our fifth year teaching together and we are both enthusiastic about the process. We have become good friends and better teachers because of it. We started teaching at Highland Park in 1989 (Beth) and 1990 (Jenny). One of the building administrators observed in both our classrooms and said, "Your styles are a lot alike. Have you ever thought about teaching together?" We had planned together for two years developing daily lesson plans, field trips, and parent letters, but we didn't realize we could teach together. We decided to try it and we have been doing it ever since. We did a presentation on collaborative

teaching at a professional conference and wrote a journal article about it (Swanson and Hootman, 1995). We've helped other teachers who wanted to collaborate to set up their classrooms. We received our Masters' degrees in 1995 with a joint culminating project.

We've tried our teaching different ways. We've had first and second graders together, and all first graders, like this year. For several years we each took responsibility for all the children. They viewed both of us as their teachers. We graded a different half of the work each night so we would be aware of all the students. We did report cards together and conducted conferences with fifty-five parents. It was really good, but some things were overwhelming. It is easier to focus on what twenty-four kids are doing on a project, rather than think about fifty-five kids.

Our classroom this year is very large. The accordion fold wall could be pulled across the middle of the room to divide it into two complete classrooms, each with its own restroom. We have several computers, a housekeeping corner with clothes for imaginary play, a science shelf to explore, a block corner for construction play, and a large classroom library of approximately 2,000 trade books. We have an *ABC* shelf loaded with magnet letters, manipulatives, and pictures that go with sounds.

The layout of the room is based on our philosophy of teaching and learning. We label everything in our room so children realize print has meaning and so they can use those words. A child might write *I used yarn on my mural* and everything might be invented spelling except for the word *yarn* because he knew to go to the yarn box and find the word on the label. We use speech bubbles (like comic books use for dialogue). We write down what class members say in speech bubbles and add them to displays like our birthday chart to emphasize the children's language and to show what they say can be written down and you write it a certain way. As a team we value children's work and put it on display in our room and in the hall. Students revisit their work and notice the work of other children.

We believe in community. Our classroom belongs to all of us, so we have baskets and bins of art supplies, crayons, markers, and pencils that we all share. Access to materials and supplies is crucial when students are expected to work independently and be responsible. The students choose where they want to sit at the tables. We try to give them the freedom to explore the room and find the answers that they're looking for.

We encourage talk. We think language is a bridge to reading and writing. We continually ask children to verbalize their thinking processes. By articulating their thinking, they bring it to a level of consciousness. A generous wait time after questions shows we believe in the children's ability to answer if they are given enough time to think about it and communicate. We try to listen to their responses with dignity and respect. What the children say is important.

Another of our values is cooperation and collaboration. It's a natural process in here because the two of us work together, and the children see that. We support children helping other children. They need opportunity to talk and solve problems with each other. They're not necessarily always on the same level, but there's so much learning and teaching going on among peers and friends. We did a great deal of buddy work when we had second and first graders together. And even with the classroom having just first graders, we find there are all levels.

We are facilitators creating contexts in which children can succeed. The students are responsible for their own learning and opportunities for success. Most of the time we combine our classes for instruction. Sometimes one of us instructs the large group, sometimes we co-teach. We take advantage of having two teachers to do role-playing to demonstrate how the children should interact. Our large group meetings include read alouds several times a day, reading or writing demonstrations, sharing, or descriptions of the work for the day, and current projects. A long general work time (one to two hours) usually occurs in the morning and afternoon. The students work on their daily assignments and projects while we work with small groups of children for guided reading and have individual writing conferences. After work time we share. Sharing is a valuable tool because it provides a reason for why we're doing this: there's an audience.

Bibliography

Adams, M., B. Foorman, I. Lundberg, and T. Beeler. 1998. *Phonemic Awareness in Young Children*. Baltimore, MD: Paul H. Brookes.

Bear, C.R., M. Invernizzi, S. Templeton, and F. Johnston. 2000. *Words Their Way: Word Study for Phonics, Vocabulary, and Spelling Instruction*. Upper Saddle River, NJ: Merrill.

Clay, M. 1993. *An Observation Survey of Early Literacy Achievement*. Portsmouth, NH: Heinemann.

Clay, M. 1993. *Reading Recovery: A Guidebook for Teachers in Training*. Portsmouth, NH: Heinemann.

Cunningham, P. M. 1990. "The Names Test: A Quick Assessment of Decoding Ability." *The Reading Teacher* **44**: 124–129.

Dahl, K., and P. Scharer. 2000. "Phonics Teaching and Learning in Whole Language Classrooms: New Evidence from Research." *Reading Teacher* **53** (7): 584–594.

Dahl, K., P. Scharer, L. Lawson, and P. Grogan. 1999. "Phonics Instruction and Student Achievement in Whole Language First-Grade Classrooms." *Reading Research Quarterly* **34** (3): 312–341.

Fisher, B. 1991. *Joyful Learning*. Portsmouth, NH: Heinemann.

Flanagan, A. 1997. "NCTE Members Pass Resolutions During Convention in Detroit: On Phonics as a Part of Reading Instruction." *Council-Grams* **61**: 5.

Galda, L. 1990. "Children's Literature as a Language Experience." *The New Advocate* **3** (4): 247–260.

Ganske, K. 2000. *Word Journeys: Assessment-Guided Phonics, Spelling, and Vocabulary Instruction*. New York: Guilford.

Goodman, Y. 1985. "Kidwatching: Observing Children in the Classroom." In *Observing the Language Learner*, ed. A. Jaggar and M. R. Smith-Burke, 9–18. Urbana, IL and Newark, DE: NCTE and IRA.

Holdaway, D. 1979. *Foundations of Literacy*. Portsmouth, NH: Heinemann.

"IRA takes a stand on phonics." 1997. *Reading Today* **14**: 1.

Moustafa, M. 1997. *Beyond Traditional Phonics: Research Discoveries and Reading Instruction*. Portsmouth, NH: Heinemann.

Opitz, M. 2000. *Rhymes & Reasons*. Portsmouth, NH: Heinemann.

Pinnell, G. S., and I. C. Fountas. 1998. *Word Matters*. Portsmouth, NH: Heinemann.

Snow, C., M. S. Burns, and P. Griffin, eds. 1998. *Preventing Reading Difficulties in Young Children*. Washington, DC: National Academy Press.

Swanson, B., and J. Hootman. 1995. "Collaboration in Action." *Ohio Journal of the English Language Arts* **36** (1): 53–57.

Strickland, D. 1998. *Teaching Phonics Today: A Primer for Educators*. Newark, DE: IRA.

Wilde, S. 1997. *What's a Schwa Sound Anyway?* Portsmouth, NH: Heinemann.

Children's Books Cited

Allen, P. 1983. *Who Sank the Boat?* New York: Coward-McCann.

At the Zoo. 1979. Glenview, IL: Scott, Foresman.

Bennett, J. 1987. *Noisy Poems*. Oxford: University Press.

Cowley, J. 1988. *The Biggest Cake in the World*. Katonah, NY: Richard C. Owen.

Drew, D. 1988. *Somewhere in the Universe*. Crystal Lake, IL: Rigby.

Edwards, P.D. 1995. *Four Famished Foxes and Fosdyke*. New York: HarperCollins.

Edwards, P.D. 1996. *Some Smug Slug*. New York: HarperCollins.

Elting, M., and M. Folsom. 1980. *Q Is for Duck*. New York: Houghton Mifflin.

Gardner, B. 1986. *Have You Ever Seen...? An ABC Book*. New York: Dodd, Mead.

Gwynne, F. 1976. *A Chocolate Mousse for Dinner*. New York: Simon & Schuster.

Gwynne, F. 1988. *The King Who Rained*. New York: Simon & Schuster.

Jonas, A. 1997. *Watch William Walk*. New York: Greenwillow.

Keats, E. J. 1962. *The Snowy Day*. New York: Viking Press.

Lindbergh, R. 1997. *The Awful Aardvarks Go to School*. New York: Putnam.

Lionni, L. 1969. *Alexander and the Wind-Up Mouse*. New York: Pantheon.

Maestro, G. 1986. *What's a Mite Might?* New York: Clarion.

Martin, B. 1991. *Polar Bear, Polar Bear, What Do You Hear?* New York: Henry Holt and Company.

McMillan, B. 1995. *Puffins Climb, Penguins Rhyme*. San Diego, CA: Gulliver.

McMillan, B. 1991. *Play Day: A Book of Terse Verse*. New York: Holiday House.

McMillan, B. 1990. *One Sun: A Book of Terse Verse*. New York: Holiday House.

McMillan, B. 1989. *The Alphabet Symphony: An ABC Book*. New York: Apple Island.

McMillan, B. 1982. *Puniddles*. Boston, MA: Houghton Mifflin.

Nelson, J. 1992. *The Baby Who Got All The Blame*. Cleveland, OH: Modern Curriculum Press.

Nelson, J. 1992. *When It Snows*. Cleveland, OH: Modern Curriculum Press.

Obligado, L. 1983. *Faint Frogs Feeling Feverish*. New York: Puffin.

Pallotta, J. 1991. *The Furry Alphabet Book*. Watertown, MA: Charlesbridge.

Pallotta, J. 1989. *The Bird Alphabet Book*. Watertown, MA: Charlesbridge.

Pallotta, J. 1989. *The Flower Alphabet Book*. Watertown, MA: Charlesbridge.

Pallotta, J. 1986. *The Icky Bug Alphabet Book*. Watertown, MA: Charlesbridge.

Peek, M. 1985. *Mary Wore Her Red Dress and Henry Wore His Green Sneakers.* New York: Clarion.

Roberts, L. 1985. *Mitt Magic: Finger Plays for Finger Puppets.* Beltsville, MD: Gryphon House.

Root, P. 1998. *One Duck Stuck.* Cambridge, MA: Candlewick.

Sabuda, R. 1994. *The Christmas Alphabet.* New York: Orchard.

Seuss, Dr. 1996. *My Many Colored Days.* New York: Knopf.

Slate, J. 1997. *Miss Bindergarten Gets Ready for Kindergarten.* New York: Penguin Putnam.

Ward, C. 1988. *Cookie's Week.* New York: Putnam.

Westcott, N. 1980. *I Know an Old Lady Who Swallowed a Fly.* Boston: Little Brown.

Wood, A. 1992. *Silly Sally.* New York: Harcourt Brace Jovanovich.

Index

Moore, Candace (*continued*)
    shared reading, examples of, 83–84
    sounding out words, example of, 5–6
    teacher-to-teacher comments, 50–51
Mutual focus, attaining, 32–33

Name charts, 65–66
Names Test (Cunningham), 21
Nursery rhymes, recommended collections, 97–98

Observation Survey (Clay), 22
Onsets, 53, 91
Orlich, Linda
    individual phonics instruction, examples of, 6, 30
    pointing strategy, 56
    reinforcement strategies, 52
    teacher-to-teacher comments, 62–63

Pattern awareness
    big books and, 79
    reinforcing, 56–57, 59, 76
    rhyming studies, 4–5, 66, 70, 79
Pattern charts, 59
Peer-learning, 3–4
Phoneme segmentation, 7
Phonemic awareness, promoting, 7, 37–39
Phonics assessments, daily
    first-grade classroom example, 22–23
    guidelines for struggling students, 40–49, 50–51
    kidwatching activities, 12–14
    reading conferences, 16–17
    running records, 14–16
    tools for, 11–12
    writing conferences, 17–18
Phonics assessments, periodic
    benchmark books, 21
    first-grade classroom example, 22–23
    Names Test, 21
    Observation Survey, 22
    scheduling of, 18–19
    spelling reviews, 19–21
    writing sample analysis, 19, 20
Phonics instruction
    guiding principles, 1–4
    handling complex letter-sound relationships, 58–59

    handling miscues, 55–56
    integrating meaning with, 53, 89
    integrating with reading and writing, 62–63, 100
    strategies, for students, 2–3, 24–27, 57–58, 61–62
    during writing workshop, 101–102
    See also Teaching strategies *and contributions from individual teachers*
Pleva, Alice
    rhyming patterns, lesson on, 4–5
    shared reading, examples of, 78, 80
    teacher-to-teacher comments, 86–87
Poetry
    as instructional tool, 4–5, 6, 77, 94–98, 100
    recommended anthologies/collections, 68–69, 96
    for shared reading, 78–79, 82
    for word study, 68–69
Pointing strategy, 56
Primary Spelling Inventory, 21
Print, enlarged, working with, 78–79
Project work
    developing/choosing projects, 124–125, 127
    phonics assessments during, 122–124
    responding to projects, reflection, 128–129
    teacher assessments of, 129–132
    teaching research skills, 126
    writing activities resulting from, 132–136
Project rings, 126–127

Re-reading, importance of, 55
Read alouds, 35, 86, 89–94
    literature studies, 91
    phonics assessment during, 13
Reading conferences, phonics assessment during, 10, 16–17
Reading, independent, 10, 59, 76
Reading instruction
    demonstrations, 61
    documenting achievement, 21–22, 62–63
    integrating phonics instruction with, 2, 62–63
Reading, shared and whole group, 87
    advantages of, 77, 85
    big books for, 79–82